The Little B[ook of] Sound Ideas

Bringing an understanding of sound and
music to all areas of learning

Written by
Judith Harries

Illustrations by Martha Hardy

Little Books with **BIG**ideas®

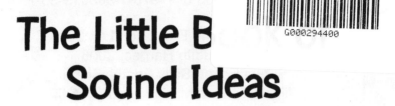

The Little Book of Sound Ideas
ISBN 1 905019 55 6 • 978-1-905019-55-7

First published in the UK, March 2006

'Little Books' is a trade mark of Featherstone Education Ltd

Published in the United Kingdom by
Featherstone Education Ltd
44 - 46 High Street
Husbands Bosworth
Leicestershire
LE17 6LP

Printed in the UK on paper produced in the European Union from managed, sustainable forests

Contents

Focus of the page   page number

Introduction
    Using this book   5   to   6
    Links with the Early Learning Goals   7   to   8

Making Sounds
    Voice Sounds   9   to   10
    Body Sounds   11   to   12
    Sound Makers   13   to   14
    Tapping Sounds   15   to   16
    Shaking All Over   17   to   18
    Scraping it Together   19   to   20
    Blowing in the Wind   21   to   22
    Plucking Sounds   23   to   24
    Opposite Sounds   25   to   26
    Sound Patterns   27   to   28

How Does it Work?
    Sound Waves   29   to   30
    Ears Hear   31   to   32
    Listen Here and Hear   33   to   34
    Sound Circles   35   to   36
    Sound Trek   37   to   38

Sounds Around
    Day and Night Sounds   39   to   40
    Outside Sounds   41   to   42
    Autumn Sounds   43   to   44
    Winter Sounds   45   to   46
    Spring Sounds   47   to   48
    Summer Sounds   49   to   50
    Weather Sounds   51   to   52
    Animal Sounds   53   to   54
    Machine Sounds   55   to   56

Around the World
    African Sounds   57   to   58
    Caribbean Sounds   59   to   60
    Chinese Sounds   61   to   62

Storing Sounds
    Sound Symbols   63   to   64
    Soundscapes   65   to   66
    Making Sound Boxes   67   to   68
    Sound Corner   69   to   70
    Recording Studio   71   to   72

More with Sounds
    Sounds and Words   73   to   74
    Sounds and Numbers   75   to   76
    Sounds in a Book   77   to   78
    Sounds with Moves   79   to   80

Resources   81   to   84

Introduction

The activities and songs in this book aim to explore the world of sound and its effect on children's learning. They will support learning in creative development through musical activities and singing. The relationship between music and other areas of the curriculum will also be explored as music helps children to develop many skills that are transferable to other subjects.

As the children play the musical games they will learn to take turns, work together co-operatively and develop personal and social skills. Singing songs and repeating rhymes develops their speaking and language skills. Listening to and discriminating between sounds aids children's ability to concentrate and respond to what they hear. Moving with imagination and co-ordination in response to sounds and playing different instruments helps to develop children's bodies and minds. There are also many opportunities to investigate sound, to ask questions and make discoveries about how, where and why sound is produced.

The Little Book of Sound Ideas

This book is divided into six sections starting with Making Sounds. This section concentrates on using voice, body and instruments and explores all the different ways sounds can be made such as tapping, shaking, scraping, blowing and plucking.

The next section is How Does it Work?, which looks at how sound is produced and how we hear sounds. It includes a key activity called Sound Circles, in which many of the other games are set, and opens the children's ears to listening to silence and sounds.

Sounds Around focuses on sounds that children may hear around them at different times of the day or year. The activities encourage children to be aware of the rich variety of sounds in their environment and challenges them to hear sounds, reproduce them and sing about them.

The activities in Around the World take the children's investigations of sound even further afield, to listen to and experiment with sounds and music from different countries.

The next section looks at different ways of Storing Sounds. The activities provide lots of ideas and resources for offering children regular opportunities to hear, use, reproduce and record interesting sounds.

The final section is More with Sounds, which looks specifically at how sound activities can inform other areas of the curriculum.

The musical activities

Each section includes ideas for musical activities for a small group of children (often seated in a circle) or for larger groups of children if appropriate. The activities are based around a stated focus or aim. At the end of each activity are some opportunities to take things further with those who are still engaged, and more activities to offer older or more mature children. The resources for each activity are clearly listed alongside the connections to the Early Learning Goals.

The songs and games

Each activity also includes at least one song, rhyme or game to further enhance learning. These songs and games are highlighted in colour within the activities and the words can be found at the bottom of the activity page. The songs are all based on familiar tunes. This should boost your confidence, the secret ingredient of all good music teaching!

The songs are short so young children can pick them up easily. Repetition in the words and music helps games and songs flow naturally. Children will quickly learn to anticipate and gain even more enjoyment from the activities.

Well-known modern and traditional songs are also suggested in some activities. If you do not know the words to these songs then you will be able to find them in many of the song and rhyme books that are suggested in the resources section.

The resources section also offers suggestions on where you can get hold of instruments, recorded music and other items to enhance the activities.

Choosing songs

* Remember, choose songs without too many words and with plenty of repetition.
* Choose songs with a narrow vocal range and avoid big jumps.
* Vary the mood and tempo.
* Add actions.
* Always count the children in on the starting note or sing the phrase 'time to sing' before you start.
* Have fun with songs and sounds.

Links with the Early Years Foundation Stage

Relevant Early Learning Goals accompany each activity in this book to help you with your planning and assessment. A full list of the goals in this book are detailed below. The extent and range of goals listed illustrates how truly cross curricular listening to, exploring and creating sounds can be!

PERSONAL, SOCIAL & EMOTIONAL DEVELOPMENT

* continue to be interested, excited and motivated to learn
* be confident to try new activities, initiate ideas and speak in a familiar group
* maintain attention, concentration and sit quietly when appropriate
* respond to significant experiences, showing a range of feelings when appropriate
* have a developing awareness of their own needs, views and feelings and be sensitive to the needs, views and feelings of others
* have a developing respect for their own cultures and beliefs and those of other people
* form good relationships with adults and peers
* work as part of a group or class, taking turns and sharing fairly
* select and use activities and resources independently

COMMUNICATION, LANGUAGE AND LITERACY

* interact with others, negotiating plans and activities and taking turns in conversations
* enjoy listening to and using spoken language, and readily turn to it in their play and learning
* sustain attentive listening, responding to what they have heard by relevant comments, questions or actions
* listen with enjoyment and respond to stories, songs, and other music, rhymes and poems and make up their own stories, songs, rhymes and poems
* extend their vocabulary, exploring the meanings and sounds of new words
    * use language to imagine and recreate roles and experiences
    * use talk to organise, sequence and clarify thinking, ideas, feelings and events
    * link sounds to letters, naming and sounding the letters of the alphabet
    * explore and experiment with sounds, words and texts
    * know that print carries meaning
    * show an understanding of elements of stories, such as main character and sequence of events
    * attempt writing for various purposes, using features of different forms such as lists, stories, instructions

PROBLEM SOLVING, REASONING AND NUMERACY

* say and use number names in order in familiar contexts
* count reliably up to 10 everyday objects
* recognise numerals 1 - 9
* in practical activities and discussion begin to use the vocabulary involved in adding and subtracting
* talk about, recognise and recreate simple patterns
* use language such as 'circle' or 'bigger' to describe the shape and size of solids and flat shapes
* use everyday words to describe position

The Little Book of Sound Ideas

KNOWLEDGE AND UNDERSTANDING OF THE WORLD

* investigate objects and materials by using all of their senses as appropriate
* find out about, and identify some features of living things, objects and events they observe
* look closely at similarities, differences, patterns and change
* ask questions about why things happen and how things work
* build and construct with a wide range of objects, selecting appropriate resources, and adapting their work where necessary
* select tools and techniques they need to shape, assemble and join the materials they are using
* find out about and identify the uses of everyday technology and use information and communication technology
* observe, find out and identify features in the place they live and the natural world
* begin to know about their own cultures and beliefs and those of other people

PHYSICAL DEVELOPMENT

* move with confidence, imagination and in safety
* move with control and co-ordination
* travel around, under, over and through balancing and climbing equipment
* show awareness of space, of themselves and of others
* recognise the changes that happen to their bodies when they are active
* use a range of small and large equipment
* handle tools, objects, construction and malleable materials safely and with increasing control

CREATIVE DEVELOPMENT

* recognise and explore how sounds can be changed, sing simple songs from memory, recognise repeated sounds and sound patterns and match movements to music
* use their imagination in art and design, music, dance, imaginative and role play and stories
* respond in a variety of ways to what they see, hear, smell, touch and feel
* express and communicate their ideas, thoughts and feelings by using a widening range of materials, suitable tools, imaginative and role play, movement, designing and making, and a variety of songs and instruments

Voice Sounds

Focus: everybody has a voice and needs to gain confidence in using it as an instrument to create sounds

Making Sounds

What you need

* CD player and nursery rhyme or other children's CDs
* lots of voices!

Early Learning Goals

PSED: be confident to try activities, initiate ideas and speak in a familiar group

CLL: link sounds to letters, naming and sounding letters of the alphabet

KUW: find out about and identify the uses of everyday technology

CD: sing simple songs from memory

Activities

* Start by encouraging all the children to hum. Choose some songs to hum, or hum along to recorded music. *When providing songs for young children remember to choose ones with a narrow vocal range and avoid big jumps (see page 6 for more help in choosing songs).*
* Learn Use Your Voice and Sing a Song (both below) - sing and hum these tunes.
* Invite all the children to hum together and then copy you when you open your mouth wide and enjoy how the sound changes.
* Experiment with lots of different letter sounds. Sing songs to la, ee, ooh, and aah. Try using consonant sounds such as tee, g, pop, s, and w.
* Experiment with different voices using the game Good Morning (see below).
* If they are still interested, play Pass a Voice Sound Around. Sit in a circle and ask each child to repeat a voice sound. Use lots of different vocal sounds, and encourage the children to start new sounds and really experiment with their voices. If children are feeling self conscious or shy, try doing it again with eyes closed!

Taking it further

* Choose some well-known songs and nursery rhymes and enjoy singing them together. If you are enthusiastic, the children will be too!

With older children...

* Choose two or three favourite voice sounds and help the children to make a pattern. Try 'squeak, squeak, whistle, pop' or 'pop, squeak, pop, squeak'.
* Play Speaking - Squeaking. Let the children experiment with how many different sorts of voices they can use. Try pairs such as speaking/squeaking, scary/wary, low/slow, growling/howling, mad/sad. Encourage the children to use contrasting voices.
* Make a recording of the children's voices talking and singing. Can they recognise themselves? Do they sound different? Who can identify the most voices?

Songs and Games

Use Your Voice

Sing to the tune of *Bobby Shaftoe*

Use your voice
and make a noise.
Humming girls
and buzzing boys.
Try to whistle
and to shout.
Use your voice
and let it out!

Use your voice
and make a noise.
Hissing girls
and laughing boys.

Try to yodel
and to sing.
Let your voice
do anything.

Can they think of different voice sounds for the girls and boys to make?

Sing a Song

Sing to the tune of *Jingle Bells*

Sing a song, sing a song,
Sing it loud and clear.
Oh what fun it is to sing,
At this time of year.
Sing a song, sing a song,
Sing it sweet and free.

Oh what fun it is to sing.
Do sing along with me!

Good Morning

Invite a small group of children to stand at one end of the room. Ask a volunteer to walk forward ten steps and stand with their back to the other children. Choose one child to say or sing 'Good morning' using their natural voice. Can the listener guess who is talking? Try again using disguised voices, opening mouth wide, speaking very slowly etc.

Body Sounds

Focus: explore body sounds and use to create actions,
patterns and accompaniments

Making
Sounds

<table>
<tr><td>

What you need

*   no special equipment

</td><td>

Early Learning Goals

PSED: continue to be interested, excited and
motivated to learn

CLL: make up their own songs, rhymes and
poems

PSRN: say and use number names in order in
familiar contexts

PD: recognise the changes that happen to their
bodies when active

</td></tr>
</table>

Activities

* Ask the children to make as many different sounds as they can with their hands - click, tap, rub, clap, slap, stroke, etc. Choose two different sounds and make a pattern eg clap clap click click. Ask the children to make up their own patterns.
* Collect together as many sounds made with their feet as possible - stamp, rub, slide, tap, etc. Use these sounds to make patterns. What other body sounds can the children discover (tongue clicks, slap thigh, tap cheek with mouth open)? Use these sounds in How Many Sounds? (see below).
* Pass a body pattern around the circle for everyone to echo eg 'stamp clap' or 'stamp slap stamp'.
* Use In My Ear There is a Drum (see below) or choose a well-known song - accompany the singing by playing a chosen body pattern on the beat.
* Sing If You're Happy and You Know it, or Peter Hammers with One Hammer. Make up new actions using body sounds.

Taking it further

* Sing Heads, Shoulders, Knees and Toes with the actions. Try missing out a different word each time you sing and just do the actions.
* Try dancing to recorded dance music. Encourage children to clap or tap feet to the beat.

With older children...

* Make a body percussion band. Ask half the group to stamp slowly on the beat. Help the other half to clap twice as fast. Put the two sounds together. Now try swapping over. It's a bit like rubbing your tummy and patting your head!
* Show the children a simple clapping game to play with a partner eg clap your hands together, clap your partner's right hand, clap your hands together, clap your partner's left hand. Can they make up some new patterns?

Songs and Games

In My Ear There is a Drum

Sing to the tune of Twinkle, Twinkle Little Star

In my ear there is a drum.
With my voice I like to hum.
Click my fingers, tap my toes,
Clap my hands and wiggle my nose,
Tap my knees, stamp my feet.
All these sounds can keep the beat.

How Many Sounds?

Sing to the tune of John Brown's Body

How many sounds can you make with your hands
(feet, mouth, body)?   X3
Just you wait and see.

Count the different sounds.
Who can make the most?

Sound Makers

Focus: introducing some musical instruments and different sources of sound

Making Sounds

What you need

* a selection of musical instruments, tuned and untuned percussion eg xylophone, tambourine, triangle, claves, maracas, bells, castanets, woodblocks, recorder, whistle
* home-made instruments such as pairs of pencils and rulers, bunches of keys, saucepan lids, large plastic bottle lids, empty yogurt pots

Early Learning Goals

PSED: select and use activities and resources independently

CLLD: interact with others, negotiating plans and activities and taking turns in conversation

PD: move with control and co-ordination

CD: express and communicate their ideas, thoughts and feelings by using a variety of musical instruments

Activities

* Set out a few instruments or sound makers for the children to explore. They need lots of opportunities to experiment freely with the sounds they can make. This should be fairly unstructured but you will need to ensure that children use the instruments carefully and with respect. Inevitably there will be some noise, so you may like to devise a signal for quietening down or ending a session!

* Sit in a circle and put out enough instruments in the centre for each child. Pass a bean bag or toy around the circle as you sing to the tune of *Pease Pudding Hot*:

> Sounds to be made, no time to lose,
> Which of these sounds shall I choose?

* Whoever is holding the bean bag or toy at the end of the song chooses a favourite instrument to demonstrate to the group. Having played they should put their chosen instrument down on the floor in front of them.

* When everybody has an instrument try playing them all together! Then try using Our Band and Five Sound Makers (see below) to encourage the children to play separately and on cue.

Taking it further

* Introduce some simple conducting signals for stopping and starting. Try holding your hands palms upwards to start the sounds. Turn your hands over and clench your fists to stop. Ask the children to take turns conducting the group as they all play together. How quickly can everyone stop? Does everybody remember to watch the conductor?

* Ask the 'conductor' to choose individual instruments or sound makers to play on their own. Encourage careful watching and listening.

With older children...

* Develop conducting skills by introducing signals for varying dynamics or loud and quiet. When your hands are far apart the sound should be loud. As your hands get closer together the sound should get quieter.

* Choose an instrument and explore how many different sounds it can make. Pass it round the circle and invite each child to make a different sound.

Songs and Games

Our Band

Sing to the tune of *Old MacDonald*

__(name of setting or your name)__ had a band,
E I E I O,
And in that band there were some tambourines,
E I E I O,
With a shake shake here and a shake shake there,
Here a shake, there a shake, everywhere a shake shake.

_____ had a band,
E I E I O.

Five Sound Makers

Sing to the tune of *Ten green bottles*

Five sound makers standing in a row,   X2
And if one sound maker should make a sound
and go (make a sound),
There'd be four sound makers standing in a row...

The Little Book of Sound Ideas

Tapping Sounds

Focus: introduce different ways of making sounds
and relate it to playing musical instruments

Making Sounds

What you need

* a selection of musical instruments to tap such as claves, drums, tambourines, woodblock, castanets, triangles
* matching pairs of coloured wooden bricks, tops from fabric softener bottles or large aerosols, rulers, kitchen roll tubes

You could ask a friendly carpenter to make wooden shapes such as fish or birds to tap together.

Early Learning Goals

CLLD: explore and experiment with sounds, words and texts

KUW: investigate objects and materials by using all of their senses as appropriate

PD: use a range of small and large equipment

CD: recognise repeated sounds and sound patterns and match movements to music

Activities

* Talk about where you might hear tapping sounds such as someone knocking on your door, footsteps, a branch tapping the window, a bird pecking, hammering, feet tapping to music.
* Make tapping sounds around the setting. Ask the children to take turns tapping different surfaces and objects. How do the sounds vary? Does the sound change if they use their knuckles rather than fingertips? Make sure that they follow the important rule: only tap yourself or things, not other people!
* Which musical instruments can you tap? Make a selection of tapping sounds. Use these sounds to accompany **Join the Tapping Team** (see below).
* Tap a rhythm pattern on your hand or an instrument for the children to copy. Invite the children to invent a tapping pattern for others to copy. Choose an instrument to play the pattern on.
* Help children to tap or clap the rhythm of their name, eg John: I Megan: I I Christopher: I I I. Play **Guess Who's Coming to Play?** (see below).

Taking it further

* Make and play home-made tappers using pairs of wooden bricks, plastic tops and lids, wooden sticks or empty tubes. Use them to accompany **Tap Tops Together**.
* Design drums using different sized wide-mouthed containers. Make the skin by stretching a deflated balloon over the opening and fastening with rubber bands.

With older children...

* Introduce tuned percussion instruments such as xylophones and metallophones. Tap with beaters and make high and low sounds.

Songs and Games

Join the Tapping Team
Sing to the tune of *Wind the Bobbin Up*

Join the tapping team,   X2
Tap, tap, tap tap tap.
Tap near the ceiling,
Tap near the floor,
Tap near the window,
Tap near the door.
Clap your hands together, 1, 2, 3.
Tap your hands upon your knee.

Guess Who's Coming to Play?

Invite two children with different names to go outside the door. Choose one to tap the rhythm of their name onto the door. Can the children inside guess which child is knocking to come and play?

Tap Tops Together
Sing this song to the tune of *We All Clap Hands Together*

Let's tap the tops/bricks/rulers together,   X3
As children like to do.

Shaking All Over

Focus: investigate sound makers and instruments
that you can make and shake to create sounds

Making Sounds

What you need

* a variety of shakers *eg* maracas, bells, tambourines
* lengths of string
* beads, buttons, pasta, shells
* lots of different plastic containers with lids and dry materials for making shakers
* shallow tray, spoons and funnels

Early Learning Goals

KUW: select the tools and techniques they need to shape, assemble and join materials they are using

PD: move with control and co-ordination

CD: express and communicate their ideas, thoughts and feelings by using a widening range of materials, designing and making musical instruments

Activities

* Choose a selection of instruments that make a sound when you shake them, such as maracas, tambourines, bells, rattles, home-made shakers, keys. How many different sounds can the children make?
* Use the shakers to play **King of the Shakers** and accompany **Shaking the Shakers** (see below).
* Thread coloured beads, buttons, cubes, shells or pasta onto lengths of string or garden wire and create shaker bracelets and anklets, mobiles or wind chimes.
* Fill shallow trays with dry lentils, rice, pasta, coins, pebbles or buttons. Provide lots of different sized plastic bottles with lids, film canisters and other small containers, and spoons and funnels. Encourage the children to make a collection of home-made shakers.
* Form a shaker band and play along to some favourite songs. Try to play on the beat or pulse. Then try to play on the offbeat eg sh shake sh shake (sh = quiet!).

Taking it further

* Make your own maracas by putting a few dried beans or grains of rice into a deflated balloon. Carefully half-inflate the balloon and cover with layers of papier mache. Attach a cardboard tube as a handle. When dry decorate with paint and varnish.
* Grow some natural shakers by planting gourd seeds and leaving the fruit to grow and then dry out. The seeds inside should make a lovely rattle sound.

With older children...

* Play *Shake, Rattle and Roll* using the shakers. Choose a different way to play or another instrument for each word such as <u>shake</u> - one shake of the maraca, <u>rattle</u> - shake the bells, <u>roll</u> - turn the tambourine around. Develop this into a dance or movement activity: <u>shake</u> - shake arms (and shakers) in the air, <u>rattle</u> - jump up and down, <u>roll</u> - forward roll.
* Make a tambourine using a paper or plastic plate, garden wire and bottle tops.
* Play *Shake Account* and guess how many items are in the shaker. Fill a small clear jar with coloured sweets, raisins or marbles. Shake about and estimate the number in the jar. The nearest guess wins the content!

Songs and Games

King of the Shakers

Sit in a circle and invite a child to sit in middle and be the King or Queen. Place a variety of shakers behind their back and ask him/her to close their eyes tight. Choose another child to creep up and try to take one of the shakers away without waking the King/Queen. Can the King/Queen tell which shaker is missing by looking or listening?

Shaking the Shakers

Sing to the tune of *Waltzing Matilda*

Shaking the shakers, shaking the shakers,
Who'll come a shaking the shakers with me?
Make a shaking sound,
Shake it all around,
Who'll come a-shaking the shakers with me?

Scraping it Together

Focus: explore making sounds by scraping materials together

Making Sounds

What you need

* a selection of things that make sounds when scraped together - corrugated cardboard, ridged plastic bottles, soap boxes, sandpaper blocks, hessian and other textured fabric
* wooden guiro

Early Learning Goals

CLLD: extend their vocabulary, exploring the meaning and sounds of new words

KUW: build and construct with a wide range of objects, selecting appropriate resources

PD: handle tools, objects, construction materials safely and with increasing control

Activities

* Try rubbing hands together to create different rhythm patterns using long and short sounds. Do rubbing patterns for the children to copy.
* Find anything that makes a good sound when you scrape it - corrugated cardboard, plastic ridged bottles, soap boxes, etc. Allow time for children to explore and experiment with different materials.
* Play Scrape the Guiro (see below). Introduce this Latin American instrument traditionally made from a gourd or wood that makes a scraping sound when scratched with the stick. If the children are enjoying this instrument you can also play Team Guiro.
* Go outside and scrape a variety of different surfaces - sweep the floor, brush the brick wall, scrape the stones together, pull sticks along fences, slide feet around, and listen to all the different sounds. Use Sweep to the Beat to accompany this activity.

Taking it further

* Listen to *Sandpaper Ballet* by Leroy Anderson (see resources page 82).
* Make a homemade guiro using a length of bamboo with indents cut into it. Scrape with a pencil or piece of doweling.

With older children...

* Demonstrate scraping sounds by using a violin or cello bow across a string on a guitar or other stringed instrument or the edge of a suspended metal cymbal.
* Make activity sound centres using materials with different textures to scrape with fingers or lolly sticks. Cover strips of stiff cardboard or plywood with different materials such as corrugated cardboard, different grades of sandpaper, bubble wrap, velvet, lace or netting, silver foil. Alternatively cover all six sides of a wooden cube or empty square box. Experiment with different sounds.

Songs and Games

Scrape the Guiro
Sing to the tune of *The Liver Birds*

Scrape the guiro, scrape the guiro, scrape the guiro,
Scrape, scrape, scrape.
Scrape the guiro, scrape the guiro,
What sound can the guiro make?

Sweep to the Beat
Sing to the tune of *Little Brown Jug*

Sweep the floor, move the broom,
Back and forth and clean the room.
Listen to it swish and say,
'I'm chasing all the dust away'.

Team Guiro
Sing to the tune of *A Sailor Went to Sea, Sea, Sea*

Oh listen to the scrape, scrape, scrape,
That my guiro can make, make, make,
So copy now the scrape, scrape, scrape,
And you can join in too. *(point to a new child to join in at the end of each verse)*

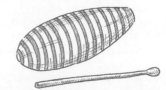

Blowing in the Wind

Focus: discover how wind can make lots of different sounds

Making Sounds

What you need

* plastic, metal or wooden wind blowing instruments or toys
* baby wipes to clean the instruments after each child
* basket of plastic bottles without lids, all different sizes
* recordings of wind and/or brass instruments
* plastic combs and greaseproof paper

Early Learning Goals

PSED: work as part of a group, taking turns and sharing fairly

KUW: ask questions about why things happen and how things work

CD: recognise and explore how sounds can be changed, and sing simple songs from memory

The Little Book of Sound Ideas

Activities

* Choose a favourite song or nursery rhyme to whistle along to. You could learn Whistle While You Work and then use it's tune to whistle or hum to.
* Make a collection of simple wind or blowing instruments such as whistles, party blowers, recorders, ocarinas, panpipes, mouth organs for the children to experiment with. Provide cleaning wipes so children can clean them after use.
* Demonstrate blowing across the end of a tube or bottle to make the column of air wobble or vibrate. Provide a basket of small empty plastic bottles for the children to try and copy you. Who can make the longest sound?
* Listen to recordings of wind or brass instruments such as flute, panpipes, clarinet, saxophone, trumpet, bassoon, tuba, etc.
* Make a class set of kazoos. Ask each child to bring in a plastic comb from home. Cut lengths of greaseproof paper to fit the combs. Fold the paper over the teeth edge of the comb and hold it loosely. Place the comb between the lips and try humming a tune. The paper should vibrate and create a familiar buzzing sound. It also tickles and causes much hilarity!

Taking it further

* Invite a musician to come into your setting and play a live wind instrument to the children.
* Make tube kazoos. Fit a piece of greaseproof paper over one end of a cardboard tube and secure it with a rubber band. Blow or hum in to the open end and the kazoo should buzz. Decorate the tubes with paint and felt pens.

With older children...

* Create bottle pipes. Collect a set of five plastic bottles and add different amounts of coloured water to them. Arrange the bottles in order and play them by blowing across the opening. Talk about how the note or pitch changes by adding water. Sing Five Wind Bottles.

Songs and Games

Whistle While You Work
Sing to the tune of *Whistle While You Work*

Whistle while you work, (whistle)
Make a sound, all around,
Blowing through the air.
Whistle while you work, (whistle)
Make a sound, all around,
Blowing everywhere.

Five Wind Bottles
Sing to the tune of *Ten Green Bottles*

Five wind bottles standing in a row.
Five wind bottles standing in a row.
Choose a wind bottle and give the top a blow.
Listen to the sound, is it high or low?

Plucking Sounds

Focus: explore making sounds using strings and string instruments

Making Sounds

What you need

* a real string instrument such as a violin, guitar or banjo
* tissue or shoe boxes and different sizes of elastic bands
* collection of junk materials - boxes, cardboard, strings, staples, drawing pins, scissors, glue, etc
* recordings of string instruments

Early Learning Goals

PSED: form good relationships with adults and peers

KUW: select the tools and techniques they need to shape, assemble and join materials they are using

PD: use a range of small and large equipment.

CD: use their imagination in art and design

Activities

* Look at a string instrument with the children. Demonstrate how sounds are produced by plucking the string and causing it to vibrate.
* Make instant string instruments using elastic bands and empty tissue boxes and encourage the children to investigate these freely.
* Make some Highly Strung Art - work together to produce giant interactive string sculptures on a display board using string or elastic bands attached over cut out shapes, junk materials, paintings and drawings of string instruments. Use lots of different textures and materials. If possible stretch the strings taut so they can be plucked and make a variety of sounds.
* Listen to an assortment of string music played on violins, cellos, basses, string orchestras, electric guitars, acoustic guitars, Spanish guitars, harps, banjos, sitars, mandolins, Chinese lutes, etc.

Taking it further

* Invite musicians to come and perform on string instruments for the children.
* Try making more string instruments using empty shoe boxes, old picture frames, and old tennis rackets with the mesh removed. Attach strings using nylon fishing line, twine, string, guitar strings or elastic bands.
* Make a one-string tea chest bass using a large box, broom handle and a length of string.
* Learn Strings Go Twang (see below) and perform it using your new instruments!

With older children...

* Talk about high and low pitch. Experiment with the thickness of elastic bands and create different pitches. Alter the length of strings and change the pitch.
* Create a string band using the homemade instruments. Start with a walking bass line saying 'dunk, dunk, dunk, dunk' to a regular beat. Add the other string sounds on top. Record the sounds and listen back.

Songs and Games

Strings Go Twang

Sing to the tune of *Mary, Mary Quite Contrary*

Twang, twang, twang, listen to the band.
Listen to the strings go twang.
Slide up and down,
And hear the sound.
Listen to the strings go twang.

Opposite Sounds

Focus: exploring musical contrasts and opposites

Making Sounds

What you need

* a large space
* a drum
* a variety of musical instruments and sound makers

Early Learning Goals

PSED: maintain attention, concentrate and sit quietly when appropriate

CLLD: make up their own stories, songs, rhymes and poems

KUW: look closely at similarities, differences, patterns and change

PD: show awareness of space, of themselves and of others

Activities

* Talk with children about sound opposites such as quiet and loud, long and short, fast and slow, high and low. Have fun demonstrating them using voices, body percussion and instruments. Invite older children to work in pairs to create opposite sounds.
* Try singing songs in different ways. Sing a lullaby such as *Rock a Bye Baby* very fast or loudly and *Here we go Round the Mulberry Bush* very slowly!
* Explore loud and quiet sounds. Ask the children to use their voices to whisper and shout. Play loud and quiet sounds on a drum. Use these drum sounds in Oh Can You Play the Opposite? Ask the children to stand up when they hear loud sounds and sit down when the drum is played quietly. Choose two other contrasting actions.
* Sit in a circle and give each child an instrument. Revise conducting activities (see Sound Makers on page 13). Choose signals for loud and quiet such as hands close together - play quietly, hands far apart - play loudly. Let the children practice conducting loud and quiet sounds. Can they make the change happen gradually?
* Explore fast and slow sounds. March around the room in time to a drumbeat and change the speed or tempo. Sing and play Traffic Jam (see below).

Taking it further

* Make a book of opposite sounds using photos, magazine pictures or drawings.
* Explore long and short sounds. Investigate which instruments play the longest sounds (cymbals) and shortest sounds (claves). Look at what the instruments are made from.

With older children...

* Explore high and low sounds. Choose two characters, a giant and a mouse, or an elephant and a baby, and use two contrasting voices (low and high) or sounds. Make up stories about the characters and invite the children to act them out, joining in with voices and sound effects.

Songs and Games

Oh Can You Play the Opposite?

Sing to the tune of *Aiken Drum*

Oh can you play the opposite,
The opposite, the opposite?
Oh can you play the opposite,
To my sounds?
(Play some short/quiet sounds)

Yes I can play the opposite,
The opposite, the opposite.
Yes I can play the opposite,
To your sounds!
(Play some long/loud sounds)

Traffic Jam

Sing to the tune of *The Wheels on the Bus*
Get gradually slower.

The wheels of the car go round and round,
Very fast, very fast.
The wheels of the car go round and round,
On the road.
The wheels of the car go round and round,
Not so fast, not so fast.
The wheels of the car go round and round,
Slowing down.
The wheels of the car go round and round,
Very slow, very slow.
The wheels of the car go round and round,
In the traffic jam.

Sound Patterns

Focus: using repeated and contrasting sounds to create patterns

Making Sounds

What you need

* a large space
* a variety of musical instruments and sound makers
* a drum

Early Learning Goals

CLL: explore and experiment with sounds, words and texts

PSRN: talk about, recognise and recreate simple patterns

PD: move with confidence, imagination and in safety

CD: recognise repeated sounds and sound patterns and match movements to music

Activities

* Start with some echo clapping and ask the children to copy the patterns that you clap (see Listen Here and Hear on page 33). Play and sing the Copy Cat Chant.
* Talk about making patterns using sounds and sing We Can Make a Pattern.
* Choose two contrasting sounds (voice, body percussion or instruments) and ask the children to turn them into a pattern.
* Split the group into half. Ask one half to stamp their feet and the other half to clap hands when you point at them. Create a pattern. Ask volunteers to come and have a go.
* Sit with a small group and give them each a turn to copy your drum pattern in Rum, Tum, Tum.
* Invite children to work with a partner, each with a different instrument, and choose two contrasting sounds. Play alternately and create a simple pattern. Ask the pairs to demonstrate their patterns to each other.

Taking it further

* Try making sound patterns using silences, e.g. clap [gap] clap [gap].

With older children...

* Make a Pattern Wall. Ask the children to draw, print or notate their patterns . They will need to each choose a colour, shape or symbol to represent their sound. Display the patterns at a low level and invite other children to play them.
* Choose two different sounds and movements such as triangle - jump up, claves - squat down; or shake tambourine - stretch, tap tambourine - curl up. Make up some sound and movement patterns and dances.

Songs and Games

Copy Cat Chant

Copy cat, copy cat
Can you copy this?
(Clap, tap or play a pattern for children to copy)
Copy cat, copy cat
Yes I copied that!

Rum, Tum, Tum
Sing to the tune of *This Old Man*

This old man, he played one,
He played a pattern on my drum,
With a rum, tum, tumty tum,
Listen to the drum.
Can you copy it?
Rum, tum, tum.
(Play a pattern on the drum for a child to copy)

We Can Make a Pattern
Sing to the tune of *Ring a Ring of Roses*

We can make a pattern,
We can make a pattern,
Clap, tap, clap, tap,
Now let's try again.

Sound Waves

Focus: enjoy finding out how sounds travel in waves through the air

How Does it Work?

What you need

* water trays
* pebbles or small stones
* shallow sand trays
* Slinky or long stretchy spring
* paper and pens

Early Learning Goals

PSED: work as part of a group or class, taking turns and sharing fairly

PSRN: talk about, recognise and recreate simple patterns

KUW: ask questions about why things happen and how things work

PD: move with control and co-ordination

The Little Book of Sound Ideas

Activities

* Gather a small group of children around the water tray. Give each child a small pebble. Drop the pebbles into the water one by one and watch the ripples.
* Discuss what makes the ripples happen. How do they move? What happens when the pebble is dropped from different heights or if larger/smaller pebbles are used?
* Talk about how sound travels in ripples through the air like the ripples in the water. Explain that as we can't see air we don't know the ripples are coming until they reach our ears. Sing Wobbling Waves (see below).
* Draw wave patterns or zigzags in the air for the children to copy. Sing Sound Senses (see below).
* Ask a child to stand across the room from the group and make a sound: clap, shout, tap a drum. Invite another child to run from the sound to the rest of the group making the wave pattern in the air. Do this lots of times so that all the children can take part.
* Stretch out a Slinky or long spring across the room. Give it a sharp push and pull at one end and watch it wobble like a giant sound wave. Talk about what happens and what makes it wobble. Remind them of the air waves and water ripples.

Taking it further

* Draw sound waves using fingers in shallow trays of dry sand or in the sand tray.
* Create giant sound waves inside or outside. Draw them on big pieces of paper using fat felt pens, paint them on walls with water or use scraps of coloured paper to make a mosaic pattern.

With older children...

* Make ear trumpets from cones of card so that the children can whisper secret messages. How far away can they stand and still hear each other?

    Be sure to tell the children that they must not shout in each other's ear trumpets.

Songs and Games

Wobbling Waves

Sing to the tune of *In and Out the Dusky Bluebells*

Drop the pebbles in the water,   X3
Watch the ripples round.

Watch the ripples moving quickly,   X3
Can you hear a sound?

Can you see the sound waves wobbling?   X3
Wobbling all around.

Sound Senses

Sing to the tune of *Knees Up Mother Brown*

Sound waves in the air,
Sound waves everywhere.
Can you see them? (pause) No!
Can you smell them? (pause) No!
Can you touch them? (pause) No!
Then hear them with your ear!

Ears Hear

Focus: this activity helps children to focus on their ears - simply focusing on their ears helps their listening and concentration!

How Does it Work?

What you need

* blindfold
* large drum or tambour, rice
* plastic cups or empty yogurt pots
* string, sticky tape, scissors

Early Learning Goals

PSED: be sensitive to the needs, views and feelings of others

CLLD: sustain attentive listening

KUW: select the tools and techniques they need to assemble and join materials

CD: respond in a variety of ways to what they hear

Activities

Please note: This activity involves children's ears and eyes being covered. Ensure that the children understand not to put their fingers in their ears, and be aware that some children hate wearing blindfolds.

* Sit a small group of children in a circle. Talk about how we hear sounds. Experiment with the effect that covering one or both ears with your hands has on your hearing.
* Play Describe the Sound.
* Now ask for a volunteer to sit in the middle and close their eyes or wear a blindfold. Invite another child to whisper the child's name.
* Where did the sound come from? Can they identify who whispered their name?
* Play What Can You Hear?
* Explain that inside the ear is a skin like the skin on a drum. Look at a real drum.
* Make a giant eardrum! Drop a few grains of rice onto the skin of the drum. Tap the drum and watch the rice jump up and down as the skin vibrates.
* Make a home-made telephone using a length of string and two plastic cups. When the string is pulled taut, ask one child to speak into one cup and the other to listen. Can they send each other a message?

Taking it further

* Look at the shapes and sizes of ears of different animals, such as rabbits, elephants, foxes, horses, monkeys, etc. Which animals can hear the best?
* Learn some simple sign language so children can think about how it might feel not to be able to hear sounds.

With older children...

* Look at a diagram of the inner ear. Talk about how our ears catch sound waves, which makes all the tiny bones wobble and so the eardrum vibrates.

Songs and Games

Describe the Sound

- a new version of I-Spy!

I can hear with my little ear something that sounds like ...
Or
I can hear with my little ear something beginning with s ...

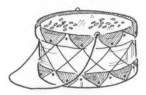

What Can You Hear?

Sing to the tune of What Shall We Do with the Drunken Sailor?

What can you hear with your little ear?
What can you hear with your little ear?
What can you hear with your little ear?
Listen to the sounds.

Solo: I can hear with my little ear...   x3
The sound of ...

Listen Here and Hear

Focus: simple copying and sound games help children to discriminate between everyday sounds and the simple instruments they hear

How Does it Work?

What you need

* screen or screened area
* 2 matching sets of instruments *eg* triangles, tambourines, pairs of claves, maracas, castanets
* large shell

Early Learning Goals

PSED: work as part of a group or class, taking turns and sharing fairly

PSRN: say and use number names in order in familiar contexts

PD: use a range of small and large equipment

CD: sing simple songs from memory, recognise repeated sounds and sound patterns

Activities

* Hide one set of instruments behind the screen. Keep the other set with you.
* Sit in a circle and play some simple copying games. Clap four times and ask the children to echo you. Make up other clapping patterns for the children to copy.
* As the children get more confident try using two sounds: tapping knees and clapping hands, or tapping shoulders and stamping feet.
* Put a selection of four or five musical instruments in the middle of the circle. Give the children time to explore the different sounds they can make.
* Learn to sing Make a Sound.
* Invite a child to go behind the screen where you hid the instruments and make a secret sound.
* Ask the other children to listen carefully. Can anyone identify the sound? Can they copy or match the sound?
* Play the Sea Shell, Sea Shell game. Ask for a volunteer to curl up small in the middle of the circle and cover their eyes. Pass the shell around the circle as you sing. Whoever is holding the shell at the end of the song, hides it behind their back and has to sing the solo line. If the child in the middle guesses correctly they win and the soloist takes their turn in the middle.

Taking it further

* Make sounds with different sound sources around the setting - tap pencils together, drum fingers on the floor, jingle keys, tear paper etc. Can the children identify the sounds?

With older children...

* See if you can make silence! Discuss the quietest and loudest places in the setting and go to the quietest place that you can gather together safely. Try not to make any sound at all. What can you still hear? (breathing, coughing, traffic sounds, footsteps).

Songs and Games

Make a Sound
Sing to the tune of *Pat-a-Cake*

Make a sound, make a sound, carefully.
Make a sound, make a sound, carefully.
Tap it or scrape it or give it a shake.
Can anyone copy the sound I make?

Sea Shell, Sea Shell
Sing to the tune of *Rain, Rain Go Away*

Sea shell, sea shell,
Listen well, can you tell
Who has got the sea shell?

Solo: I have got the
sea shell.

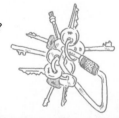

Sound Circles

Focus: using familiar circle game formats to enjoy and explore making sounds

How Does it Work?

What you need

* a selection of percussion instruments

Early Learning Goals

PSED: maintain attention, concentrate and sit quietly when appropriate

CLL: enjoy listening to and using spoken language, and readily turn to it in their play and learning

PSRN: use language such as 'circle' to describe shape of solids and flat shapes

PD: show awareness of space, of themselves and of others

Activities

* Find a quiet place to sit in a circle.
* Pass a sound around the circle. Ask each child to repeat a sound such as a hand clap or a sound word like 'bang' all round the circle. Can they do it in time to a beat?
* Clap a simple rhythm pattern and pass it round the circle.
* Help each child to choose their own vocal or body sound to make. Go round the circle listening to all the sounds one by one. Try not to repeat anyone else's sound.
* Make a Circle of Sounds. Invite each child to choose a different instrument. Take it in turns to make a sound and ask the next child to play when the previous sound ends. Try not to leave any gaps or overlap!
* Play a cumulative circle game resulting in a long list of sounds. 'I sat in a circle and made a _____ sound. I sat in a circle and made a _____ sound and a _____ sound' etc.
* Sing some circle songs or ring games such as *Here we go Round the Mulberry Bush*, *The Farmer's in His Den* and *Skip to my Lou*.

Taking it further

* At circle time, talk about favourite sounds, scary sounds, horrible sounds, comforting sounds, and so on.
* Use a piece of stretchy elasticated rope tied in a ring (available from www.jabadao.org). Ask the children to sit in a circle and hold onto the rope until it is stretched taut. Sing some rowing songs such as *Row, Row, Row Your Boat* and *The Big Ship Sails on the Alley Alley O*. This is a good activity for bonding together a new group of children. Take it in turns to sit inside the 'boat'.
* Play Chinese Whispers. Pass a simple verbal message around the circle such as 'keep smiling' or 'it's time for snack'. Does the message get round unchanged?

Songs and Games

Make a Circle Sound

Sing to the tune of *John Brown's Body*

Come and sit in the circle.   X3
And pass a sound around.
Make a circle sound.

Whistle, clap and sing,
Shout and stamp and ring,
Tap and play anything,
Make a circle sound.

More Circle Sounds

Try this new circle song to the tune of *Ring a Ring of Roses*

Ring a ring of sounds,
Dancing round and round.
Loud sounds,
Quiet sounds,
Up and down.

And for more verses try singing 'Fast/Slow sounds' or 'High/low sounds'.

Sound Trek

How Does it Work?

What you need

* paper, pencils, clipboards
* portable recording equipment or digital camera (optional)

Early Learning Goals

PSED: explore and experiment with sounds, words and texts

KUW: find out about and identify uses of everyday technology

PD: move with confidence, imagination and in safety

CD: respond in a variety of ways to what they hear

Activities

* Explain to the children that you are all going to be Sound Collectors and that the first listening walk will be around the inside of your setting. Before setting off talk with the children about sounds they might expect to hear. When you get back see how many sounds they remember hearing.

* Explain that you are now going on a walk outside the setting. What sounds do the children expect to hear outside? Encourage the children to make picture or word lists of the sounds they expect to hear.

* Sing We're Going on a Sound Trek.

* While on your trek, encourage the children to draw or write a list of sounds they actually hear. Discuss the lists when you get back. What did they hear? Did some children hear sounds that others didn't? Were any of the sounds unexpected? Compare their predictions with what they actually heard.

* Go on another walk - inside or outside - and take a tape recorder or digital camera to record some of the sounds. Can the children identify some of the recorded sounds.

Taking it further

* Set up a Sound Trek around the room. Set up sounds at different places such as a telephone ringing, talking on the radio, recorded or live music, a bird singing, a computer, a creaking door, children playing in the water tray.

* Draw maps of the sound trek showing all the sounds they found.

With older children...

* Invite the children to be Sound Detectives. Use pictures/photos and sound recordings from your treks. See if the children can match the image to the sound. These can be used for home-made Sound Bingo.

* Give the children a short list of sounds to collect. Ask them to work in pairs and collect as many sounds as possible.

Songs and Games

We're Going on a Sound Trek

Play this game based on *We're Going on a Bear Hunt*.
Say the rhyme as you go around collecting sounds.

We're going on a sound trek.
We're going to find some sounds.
What a noisy day.
Let's get going!
Oh no, listen.
It's a _____ .

Can't go over it,
Can't go under it,
Can't go round it,
Got to go through it!

We all went on a sound trek   X3
To hear what we could hear.
But all that we could hear
But all that we could hear,
Was (list sounds) _____ .
That's what we could hear.

Focus: listening to and using sounds that we hear around us in the day and night

Sounds Around

What you need

* a selection of musical instruments and sound makers
* a selection of stories about night and day

Early Learning Goals

PSED: respond to significant experiences, showing a range of feelings when appropriate

CLLD: listen with enjoyment and respond to stories

KUW: find out about and identify the uses of everyday technology

CD: use their imagination in art and design, music, imaginative and role play and stories

Activities

* Go on a mystery Sound Hunt (refer to Sound Trek on page 37). Can the children find the following: a loud sound, a quiet sound, a sound that lasts for a long time, a scary sound, an angry sound, a gentle sound, a surprising sound?
* Sing **Lying in My Bed at Night** and other songs about the night such as *Twinkle, Twinkle Little Star, Diddle Diddle Dumpling* and *Dingle-Dangle Scarecrow*.
* Talk about sounds you might hear during the day and night. Make a list of the different sounds: <u>Day</u> - laughing, talking, music playing, car engines and horns, telephone ringing, birds singing, etc. <u>Night</u> - snoring, owl hooting, dog barking, clock ticking, pipes gurgling, baby crying, footsteps, etc.
* Read a story about the night like *Newton* by Rory Tyger (Little Tiger Press) and talk about how sounds at night can be scary. Act out lying in bed at night and hearing strange sounds. Help the children to create some scary sound effects using voices, body percussion and instruments.

Taking it further

* Learn to sing some lullabies eg *Hush Little Baby* or Brahms' *Lullaby*.
* Collect pictures of day and night images from magazines and newspapers.

With older children...

* Divide into two groups and create two contrasting soundscapes of day and night sounds. Record the sounds and listen back.
* Make two contrasting pictures or posters of day and night sounds. Cut out or draw pictures of daytime sounds and stick them onto a large piece of white or light blue paper. Stick the night sounds onto a black or dark blue background.

Songs and Games

Lying in My Bed at Night
Sing to the tune of *Bobby Shaftoe*

Lying in my bed at night,
Heard a sound, such a fright.
Pull the cover to my nose,
Could it be a ghost!
[No, it's just a branch tapping on the window!]

In a Dark, Dark Wood

I See the Moon

Star Light, Star Bright

Start Your Day

Outside Sounds

Focus: exploring sounds outside and enjoying making music in the fresh air

Sounds Around

What you need

* lots of materials for making outside instruments *eg* large clear bottles, Seeds, pebbles, lengths of doweling, metal bottle tops, hammer and nails, flowerpots, string, bamboo, metal piping, garden netting, metal saucepans and lids, spoons, whisks, chains, aluminium cans and trays, bells, triangles and tambourines
* wooden spoons or sticks for beaters

Early Learning Goals

PSED: select and use activities and resources

CLLD: attempt writing for different purposes, using features of different forms such as lists, stories and instructions

KUW: build and construct with a wide range of objects, selecting appropriate resources and adapting their work where necessary

PD: move with confidence, imagination and in safety

Activities

* Enjoy a singing session outside. Choose a fine day and take the children outside. Sing lots of movement and action songs such as *The Grand Old Duke of York*, *I went to the Garden and Dug up the Ground* and *I Went to School One Morning*.
* Collect together a set of outside instruments and sound makers and store them in a plastic box. Allow the children free access to these when they play outside. Encourage them to play rhythms and accompany songs together.
* Make some special outside instruments such as large bottles filled with seeds or pebbles to scrape and shake, and jingle sticks made from lengths of broom handle with pairs of metal bottle tops attached. Make flowerpot rattles using different sized plastic pots strung together or wind chimes from lengths of bamboo or metal piping and suspend them from branches or play equipment. Help the children to write instructions on how to play their new instruments.
* Hang up a length of washing line or a piece of garden or fishing net and create a Sound Web. Attach unwanted metal pots, kitchen utensils, plant pots, chains, aluminium cans, old metal musical instruments, and corrugated plastic trays. Give the children beaters or sticks so they can tap, scrape and shake the pots to make magnificent messy music.
* While you are outside ask the children to listen to the sounds around them. Find a quiet place inside and discuss what sounds they remember hearing. Use these sounds for Outside My Window.

Taking it further

* Ask the children to choose an instrument each and walk around playing like a marching band. Sing Marching Band whilst on parade.
* Find out which instruments work best outside. How far away does the sound travel? Ask the children to test each instrument by moving away until they cannot hear it.

With older children...

* Organise an open air concert or garden party so the children can show off their outside music. Design posters to invite parents and carers to come to the event.

Songs and Games

Outside My Window

Sing to the tune of *There Was a Princess Long Ago*

Outside my window, I heard a sound,
I heard a bird, heard a bird.
Outside my window, I heard a bird,
Sounds all around.

(friend, car, siren, shout, wind, crash)

Marching Band

Sing to the tune of *The Ants Came Marching*

We're playing in a marching band,
we are, we are.   X2

Playing fast, playing slow,
Playing high, playing low.
We're playing in a marching band,
we are, we are.

Autumn Sounds

Focus: use natural Autumn materials to explore and create sounds together

Sounds Around

What you need

* baskets or bags
* access to outside area and lots of autumn materials
* large clear plastic ribbed bottles.

Early Learning Goals

PSED: have a developing awareness of their own needs, views and feelings and be sensitive to the needs, views and feelings of others

PSRN: count reliably up to ten everyday objects

KUW: find out about, & identify, some features of living things, objects and events they observe

PD: show awareness of space, of themselves and of others

Activities

* Go on an Autumn walk around the gardens or a local park. Make sure all children are wearing warm, waterproof clothes and suitable footwear. Enjoy jumping in puddles and kicking leaves. Listen to the sounds as the water splashes and the leaves scrunch underfoot.
* Collect Autumn leaves and fruits to use for sound activities back inside. Use some of the leaves as part of a dance to accompany **Autumn Leaves Are Falling** or **On an Autumn Day**.
* Make Autumn shakers. Use large clear plastic bottles filled with a selection of materials such as dry leaves, conkers, acorns, feathers, seeds, stones, etc. Which shaker makes the loudest or quietest sound?
* Talk about the sounds of fireworks. Choose three or four different fireworks eg sparkler, rocket, banger, Catherine wheel, and use voices, body percussion or instruments to create sounds. Draw a simple symbol or picture to represent each firework. Ask the children to make the sound when you point at the picture. Sing **5 4 3 2 1**.

Taking it further

* Use other natural materials such as walnuts, coconuts, gourds, bamboo and sticks to make sounds. Let children experiment with these sound makers.

With older children...

* Design a bonfire dance. Stand a small group of children in a tight circle around another group of children with instruments to make crackly sounds such as drums, maracas, plastic trays and biscuit inserts. Ask them all to rub their hands together to create the sound of the fire burning. Ask the musicians in the centre to build up the sounds as the fire burns more fiercely. Let the standing children take it in turns to dart off as the flames leap about. See *The Little Book of Dance* for more Autumn dance ideas.

Songs and Games

Autumn Leaves Are Falling

Sing to the tune of *I Can Sing a Rainbow*

Red and yellow,
And orange and brown,
Leaves are changing now.
Autumn leaves are falling,
Leaves are falling,
Falling to the ground.

On an Autumn Day

Sing to the tune of *Jelly on the Plate*

Walking through the leaves,   X2
Walking, walking, walking, walking,

On an Autumn day.

Jumping in the leaves, etc.
Crunching all the leaves, etc.
Splashing in the puddles, etc.

5 4 3 2 1

5, 4, 3, 2, 1.
Count down is almost done.
The rocket zooms into the sky.
Watch it fly really high.

5, 4, 3, 2, 1.
Countdown is almost done.
The firework whizzes round and round,
Sparks fizzing to the ground.

Winter Sounds

Focus: discover sounds and songs about winter and seasonal festivals

Sounds Around

What you need

* extra adults to help you on a wintry walk
* gloves and mittens
* metal instruments

Early Learning Goals

PSED: have a developing respect for their own cultures & beliefs & those of other people

KUW: look closely at similarities, differences, patterns and change

PD: handle tools, objects, construction and malleable materials safely and with increasing control

CD: respond in a variety of ways to what they see, hear, smell, touch and feel

The Little Book of Sound Ideas

Activities

* Wrap up warm and go for a wintry walk. Listen to the sounds of Winter - crunching footsteps on frosty ground, dripping water as it thaws, strong winds blowing, children sliding on the icy ground, muffled quiet when snow falls. What other sounds do the children hear that are special to winter?
* As soon as any snow falls go outside! Enjoy walking in it and listening to it crunch and scrunch under foot. Sing Take it Slow (see below).
* Try clapping with gloves and mittens on. Play echo clapping games. Does it sound the same as with bare hands?
* Use the various winter festivals such as Eid, Diwali, Hanukkah and Christmas as a stimulus for creative activities using songs and sounds.
* Listen to and sing some simple Christmas carols such as *Away in a Manger*, *Deck the Halls*, *Jingle Bells* and *Rudolph, the Red Nosed Reindeer*.
* Make some seasonal sounds using metal instruments, eg jingle bells, triangles, chime bars, glockenspiels and hand chimes.

Taking it further

* Listen to winter music: *Four Seasons* by Vivaldi, *The Nutcracker Suite* by Tchaikovsky.
* Sing **Twinkle, Twinkle Little Light** and **On Christmas Day**.

With older children...

* Create a musical year. Ask children to sit in a circle and choose a sound for each season, for instance: Winter - sleigh bells, Spring - birds singing, Summer - bouncing balls, Autumn - crunching leaves. Use voices, body percussion or instruments to make these sounds. Divide the circle into four groups, one for each season, and point at each group in turn to create the passing year!

Songs and Games

Take it Slow
Sing to the tune of *Hot Cross Buns*

Crunching snow,   X2
Stepping very carefully,
Take it slow!
Slippery slide,   X2
Stepping very carefully,
Or you'll glide!
Freezing frost,   X2
Stepping very carefully,
All's not lost!

Twinkle, Twinkle Little Light
Sing to the tune of *Twinkle, Twinkle Little Star*

Twinkle, twinkle little light.

Shining brightly in the night.
Lights to celebrate the year.
Sights to make us feel good cheer.
Twinkle, twinkle little light.
Shining brightly in the night.

On Christmas Day
Sing to the tune of *I Saw Three Ships*

I heard the bells ring and chime,
On Christmas day, on Christmas day.
I heard the bells ring and chime,
On Christmas day in the morning.

I heard the presents rustle and rip ...
I heard the children slip and slide ...
I heard the sleigh's jingling bells ...

Spring Sounds

Focus: use bird songs and calls to explore the sounds of spring

Sounds Around

What you need

* live or recorded bird songs
* pitched musical instruments
* for Musical Whirly Windmills - stiff coloured paper, rulers, scissors, pins with large heads, pencils with erasers on the end, short pieces of wooden doweling, small jingle bells, strings of beads, aluminium foil, rattles

Early Learning Goals

CLLD: listen with enjoyment and respond to stories, songs and other music, rhymes and poems and make up their own stories, songs, rhymes and poems

PSRN: in practical activities and discussion begin to use the vocabulary involved in adding and subtracting

KUW: select the tools & techniques they need to shape, assemble & join materials they use

Activities

* Talk about one of the first signs of Spring when birds begin to sing in the mornings. Ask the children to listen out at home and school for different bird songs and calls. Listen to some recorded bird song (see resources page 83 for singing bird toys).
* Sing the children's names using the simple two-note 'cuckoo' tune. Can they sing 'Hello' back to you?
* Use the cuckoo tune to sing other instructions to the children throughout the session such as 'Now it's time to eat your snack' or 'Come and hear a story'.
* Play the cuckoo call on two pitched notes, G and E on chime bars, xylophone, piano, recorder or any other available pitched instrument. Play patterns using these two notes for the children to echo sing. Older children may be able to notate the patterns using black spots above (high) or below (low) a line.
* Sing some well-known songs about Spring such as *Five Little Ducks Went Swimming One Day* and *Five Little Speckled Frogs*. Try the finger rhymes Two Green Frogs and Five Umbrellas (see below).

Taking it further

* Make up an umbrella and Wellington boots dance to *Singing in the Rain*, *Raindrops Keep Falling on my Head* or Drip Drip Drop.

With older children...

* Make a Musical Whirly Windmill. Cut out two equal size squares from two different colours of paper and stick them together. Draw diagonal lines across each square from corner to corner and cut two thirds of the way up each line. Fold alternate corners into the centre and push a pin through the middle and secure to a cardboard tube or piece of doweling. Attach beads, bells, springs cut from aluminium foil, and rattles. Try blowing on the windmill and watching it spin.

Songs and Games

Two Green Frogs
- a finger rhyme based on *Two Little Dicky-Birds*

Two little green frogs,
sitting on a bank.
One named Freddie,
one named Frank.
Hop away Freddie,
hop away Frank!
Come back Freddie,
come back Frank!
or,
Two fat grey geese ...

Five Umbrellas
Try this new finger rhyme:

5 umbrellas by the front door,
Put one down and then there were 4.
4 umbrellas under the tree,
Put one down and then there were 3.
3 umbrellas red, white and blue,
Put one down and then there were 2.
2 umbrellas waiting for the sun,
Put one down and then there was 1.
1 umbrella alone in the hall,
Put one down and that was all.

Drip Drip Drop
Sing to the tune of *Little April Showers* from Bambi

Drip, drip, drop,
Can you hear the showers?
Rain is falling all around.
Drip, drip, drop,
Falling on the flowers.
Rain is falling to the ground.
Drip, drip, drop,
Drip, drip, drop.
Drip, drip, drop,
Stop!

Summer Sounds

Focus: having fun exploring the sights, sounds and activities of Summer

Sounds Around

What you need

* holiday brochures, or paper and drawing materials
* a selection of musical instruments
* access to park, playground or climbing equipment
* half inflated balloons or light balls to use with large piece of fabric, sari, lycra or old net curtains

Early Learning Goals

PSED: form good relationships with adults and peers

CLLD: explore and experiment with sounds, words and texts

PSRN: use language such as 'circle' or 'bigger' to describe the shape and size of solids and flat shapes

PD: travel around, under, over and through balancing and climbing equipment

Activities

* Collect together ideas of Summer sounds such as children playing outside or racing on sports day, the mower cutting grass, insects buzzing, seagulls calling, waves splashing on the beach, sizzling sausages on the BBQ. Cut pictures of things that make Summer sounds from holiday brochures or draw them to make Summer scenes.
* Ask the children to use voices, body percussion or musical instruments to create these sounds and build up a sound picture of the summer as you point at each item.
* On a Summer's day, go on a visit to the local park or children's playground. March there and back singing **Sing a Song of Summer**. Use the movement and shapes of the play equipment to encourage the children to experiment with their voices: up the steps and swoop down the slide; slide the voice gently up and down on the swing; very high and very low to create the seesaw; round and round on the roundabout (use the sketches on page 84).
* Using a parachute, sari or piece of lycra, ask the children to sit in a circle and hold the edges of the fabric. Place plastic balls or half inflated balloons onto the material and bounce them into the air as you sing **Balloons Are Floating Everywhere**.

Taking it further
* Play **Snug as a Bug in a Rug**.
* Set the climbing and play equipment out as a circuit with tunnels, balance beams, slides, etc. See how many times the children can go round the circuit. Talk about high and low levels as they crawl and climb.

With older children...
* Use the names of favourite drinks and ice creams to create chants and market calls: Raspberry Lolly, 99 Cone, Orange Fizz on a stick. Use the two-note 'cuckoo' call (see Spring Sounds on page 47). Can you write a new jingle for the ice-cream van?

Songs and Games

Sing a Song of Summer
Sing to the tune of *Sing a Song of Sixpence*

Sing a song of summer,
A picnic would be fun.
Hear the children laughing,
In the summer sun.
Splashing in the water,
Swinging on the swing.
Listen to the happy sounds,
That summer time does bring.

Balloons Are Floating Everywhere
Sing to the tune of *The Wheels on the Bus*

Balloons are floating everywhere,

Everywhere, everywhere.
Balloons are floating everywhere,
In the summer sun.

or, The balls are bouncing up and down...

Snug as a Bug in a Rug
Ask for a volunteer to leave the room while you choose another child or 'bug' to hide under the picnic blanket. Ask them to make buzzing noises. Can they be identified? If the child guesses right they win and another volunteer is chosen.

You Are My Sunshine

The Sun Has Got His Hat On

Weather Sounds

Focus: have fun creating different weather conditions using sounds

What you need

* water tray
* different sized plastic bottles, trays, sieves, colanders, tubes etc
* empty plastic margarine tubs with holes pushed through
* selection of sound makers & instruments
* silver or mirrored foil cut into puddle shapes

Early Learning Goals

PSED: be confident to try activities, initiate ideas and speak in a familiar group

CLLD: use language to imagine and recreate roles and experiences

KUW: investigate objects and materials by using all of their senses as appropriate

CD: express & communicate their ideas, thoughts & feelings by using movement, & a variety of songs & musical instruments

Activities

* Talk about various types of rain. Put lots of containers in the water tray, including different sized bottles, plastic trays, sieves, tubes, pipettes, colanders, syringes, and aluminium trays. Encourage the children to make lots of watery sounds by dripping and pouring the water.
* Make your own colanders by puncturing different numbers and sizes of holes in the bottom of margarine tubs.
* Use voices, sound makers or musical instruments to create the sound of a storm. Begin with a few raindrops (random taps on claves or tongue clicks), distant rumbling thunder (tap tambour or clapping hands), flashes of lighting (triangle trills or cymbals), pouring rain (maracas, rainsticks or fingertips on table top), explosive thunder (cymbals, large sheets of cardboard to wobble or stamping feet). Can they make the storm fade away at the end?
* Cut out puddle shapes from silver or mirrored foil. Ask the children to tap rain patterns on them. Use the **Raindrops** song and increase the intensity as the rain gets heavier.
* Sing *I Hear Thunder* and add sound effects.

Taking it further

* Weather dances - use rainbow coloured ribbons tied to curtain rings and make up a dance to *I Can Sing a Rainbow*. Create a dance using **Whatever the Weather** or *A Rainy Day* (Track 2 on *Music for The Little Book of Dance*).

With older children...

* Create a musical weather forecast using different sounds for each type of weather. Sunshine - slow taps on tuned percussion, rain - maracas or rainsticks, snow - triangles and bells, windy - blow over tops of bottles, storm - tambourines, etc. Hang up a map of the country and use weather symbols. Invite the weather forecaster to point at different symbols and listen to the weather!

Songs and Games

Raindrops
Sing to the tune of *Yankee Doodle*

Raindrops dripping in the puddles,
Dripping to the ground.
Drip drop drip drop drip drop drip drop,
Listen to the sound.

Raindrops falling in the puddles,
Falling to the ground.
Pitter patter pitter patter,
Listen to the sound.

Raindrops pouring in the puddles,
Pouring to the ground.

Splishing splashing splishing splashing,
Listen to the sound.

Thunder crashing through the clouds,
It's a thunderstorm.
Crashing crashing crashing crashing,
Listen to the sound.

Whatever the Weather

Whatever the weather,
I like to go,
and play in the sun,
the rain and the snow.

Whatever the weather,
I like to stay,
outside in the wind,
to play all day.

Whatever the weather,
I like to lie,
and watch the clouds,
go floating by.

Whatever the weather,
I like to hop,
and skip and jump,
and never stop!

The Little Book of Sound Ideas

Animal Sounds

Focus: using animal sounds, songs and games

Sounds Around

What you need

* paper, card, paint, pens, etc
* recordings of animal sounds
* large space to move about
* bag of toy farm animals

Early Learning Goals

CLLD: extend their vocabulary, exploring the meaning and sounds of new words

PSRN: talk about, recognise and recreate simple patterns

KUW: find out about & identify, some features of living things, objects and events they observe

CD: use their imagination in art & design, music, dance, imaginative & role play & stories

The Little Book of Sound Ideas

Activities

* Listen to real-life recordings of animal sounds such as whale song, cicadas, wolves howling or lions roaring. Can the children recognise the different animals?
* Sit in a circle and invite each child to make a different animal sound in turn. Try not to repeat any sounds. How many different sounds can they create?
* Create an animal sounds display on the wall. Draw and paint pictures of different animals with big speech bubbles coming from their mouths containing the sounds. If possible, use recordings of the animals sounds to create an interactive display.
* Play **Buzz, Bee, Buzz**.
* Try this new version of *Beans*. Invite the children to move and make the sound of different jungle animals when you call them out: lion (stalk and roar), snake (slither and hiss), monkey (swing and 'ooh ooh'), parrot (fly and squawk), frog (jump and 'ribbit').
* Place some toy farm animals in a bag. Sing *Old MacDonald Had a Farm* or **I Went to Visit the Farm One Day** and bring out a different toy for each verse.

Taking it further

* Listen to *Carnival of the Animals* by Saint-Saens. Make up a dance to accompany it.

With older children...

* Ask the children to paint some imaginary animals or monsters and invent funny sounds for them to make. Create an alternative wall display!
* Make patterns using animal sounds. Try ' moo moo baa baa', 'cluck cluck cluck woof' or 'buzz hiss hiss, buzz hiss hiss'. Ask the children to use pictures and symbols to draw their animal sound patterns on thin strips of paper for other children to read.

Songs and Games

I Went to Visit the Farm One Day
I went to visit the farm one day,
I saw a __(cow)__ across the way.
What d'ya think I heard him say?
__(moo, moo, moo)____.

Try visiting the zoo, park or sea and substitute appropriate animals.

Buzz, Bee, Buzz
- a new version of *Squeak, Piggy, Squeak*. Sit in a circle and ask for a volunteer to wear a blindfold. Be aware that some children hate wearing blindfolds. Spin them round and let them find someone to sit on. They then say 'Buzz, Bee, buzz' and the seat has to 'buzz'. Can the blindfolded child guess who they are sitting on?

Old MacDonald Had a Farm (Traditional)

The Animal Fair (Traditional)

Machine Sounds

Focus: exploring and inventing sounds for machines

Sounds Around

What you need

* machines or recordings of machine sounds
* junk and construction material
* large space

Early Learning Goals

CLLD: explore and experiment with sounds, words and texts

KUW: build and construct with a wide range of objects, selecting appropriate resources and adapting their work where necessary

PD: travel around, under, over and through balancing and climbing equipment

CD: recognise repeated sounds and sound patterns and match movements to music

The Little Book of Sound Ideas

Activities

* Talk about the sounds that different machines make at home, at school and outside. Listen to recordings of machine sounds and identify different machines (toaster, mixer, clock, kettle, TV, computer, telephone, vacuum cleaner, mower, juicer, washing machine, tumbler drier, car, motorbike, fire engine, alarms, lorry, tractor, etc).
* Sing Hickory Tickory Tock.
* Sit in a circle and invite each child to make a machine sound. Try and play it without stopping so that the machine sounds keep coming. Then choose four good sounds and create a repeating pattern or ostinato.
* Build a giant machine using junk and construction material. Add a conveyor belt by wrapping a loop of lining paper around a slide or a length of sturdy card, so boxes can move along. Invite the children to invent sounds that the machine makes at particular points. What happens when the machine is switched off?

Taking it further

* Play Robot Master. Ask each child to find a space and freeze like an inactive robot. Go round and switch each robot on. The 'on' button can be a child's nose or toe, it's up to you! They must spring into action and obey all orders such as 'walk', 'march', 'go backwards', 'jump' or 'spin' in the style of a robot. Add sound effects. Use a whistle or drum to stop the movement. How quickly can they stop?
* Sing My Machine Starts to Hum using robot voices.

With older children...

* Collect together machine sound words (ding, crash, bang, buzz, hum, tick) and write them on pieces of card. Ask the children to work with a partner and invent a movement to go with each word. Combine the sounds and actions into a group moving machine.
* Work in groups to create junk machines using different sized boxes, bottle tops, egg cartons, corks, corrugated cardboard, aluminium foil and cardboard tubes. Ask each group to use vocal sounds, body percussion or instruments to create sound effects for their machines. Have conversations between the machines.

Songs and Games

My Machine Starts to Hum

My machine starts to hum,
Dum, dum, dah dah, dum,
My machine starts to hum,
Dah dah, dum, dit de dah,
Now it's moving very fast,
Dum, dah dah, dum, dit.
Listen, can you hear it?
Dum, dum, dum, dum,
dum, dum, dum, ching!

Hickory Tickory Tock

Hickory tickory tock,
The mouse ran up the clock.
The clock struck one,
The mouse ran down,
Hickory tickory tock.

Stickety stackety stone,
The tone rang on the phone.
The tone rang once,
The tone rang twice,
Stickety stackety stone.

Clickety clackety claw,
The bell rang on the door.
The bell rang once,
The bell rang twice,
Clickety clackety claw.

African Sounds

Focus: enjoy African drumming and rhythms and try sending messages to each other

Around the World

What you need

* African drums or homemade drums
* enough pebbles for each child in group
* large gathering drum
* recordings of African music eg *Rough Guide to the Music of West Africa* or African inspired music such as *African Greeting* (Track 5 on *Music for The Little Book of Dance*)

Early Learning Goals

PSED: work as part of a group or class

CLLD: interact with others, negotiating plans and activities and taking turns in conversation

PD: show awareness of space, of themselves and of others

CD: recognise and explore how sounds can be changed, recognise repeated sounds and sound patterns

Activities

* Sit in a circle and play these African drummer games. Start with some echo clapping (see Listen Here and Hear on page 33). Then tap a rhythm pattern on the drum and ask each child to clap it round the circle.
* Pass a small drum around the circle as you sing Come and Play. At the end of the song invite the child holding the drum to play a pattern. Ask all the children to clap the pattern back. Try this again using Gathering Drum or We're Playing on the Drum.
* Play passing games based on the African game Mancala. Start with one pebble. Ask the children to pass it to the child on their left in time to a slow regular drum beat. When they can do this add another pebble until each child has one (this is hard!).
* Try to get hold of a large drum that a group of five or six children can gather round to play together. Encourage the children to try making different sorts of sounds by bouncing their hand off the centre of the drum (bass sound) and then tapping the edge of the drum (higher sound). Use the gathering drum songs given below.

Taking it further

* In West Africa, there are talking drums that change pitch like our voices. Try having a chat using drums. Ask a child to say something using the drum instead of their mouth. Think of the words and tap the rhythm on the drum. Invite another child to answer them. They do not need to guess what the other is actually saying!

With older children...

* Talk about the natural sounds of Africa such as animals (lions, elephants, cheetahs, chimpanzees, warthogs), birds, insects, frogs, rainforest, etc. Choose sounds and create a soundscape of Africa (see Soundscapes on page 65).
* In Africa, drums called 'slit gongs', made from hollowed logs, are used to send messages from village to village. Use a wooden tongue drum, bongos or two different sized homemade drums to send messages. Choose two or three messages such as 'Help!', 'Storm coming', or 'Dinner is ready'. Invent patterns for each and pass the messages on.

Songs and Games

Come and Play
Sing to the tune of *Rain, Rain Go Away*

Come and play,   X2
My drum is talking.
Hear it say,   X2
Your drum is talking.

Gathering Drum
Sing to the tune of *Alouette*

Gather round the drum today.

Tap, tap, tap, tap,
Tap, tap, tap, tap.
Gather round the drum today.
It's your turn to stay and play.

We're Playing on the Drum
Sing to the tune of *A Hunting We Will Go*

We're playing on the drum.   X2
E I Addy Oh.
We're playing on the drum.
But now the drum says STOP!

The Little Book of Sound Ideas

Caribbean Sounds

Focus: let children enjoy finding out about another culture by listening to and exploring the sounds of the Caribbean

Around the World

What you need

* CD of music from the Caribbean
* audio or video recording of *Under the Sea* from *The Little Mermaid*
* a steel pan or a picture of one
* various sizes of empty tins such as biscuit, baby milk, coffee, hot chocolate and crisp tubes, wooden spoons
* a selection of caribbean musical instruments such as guiros, claves & maracas

Early Learning Goals

PSED: have a developing respect for their own cultures and beliefs & those of other people

CLLD: listen with enjoyment and respond to stories, songs and other music, rhymes and poems

KUW: observe, find out about and identify features in the place they live and the natural world

CD: express & communicate their ideas, thoughts & feelings by using a widening range of materials, suitable tools, designing & making, & a variety of songs & musical instruments

Activities

* Listen to some music from the Caribbean. Listen to *Under the Sea* from Disney's *The Little Mermaid* to introduce the sounds. Try recordings from the Rough Guide series, including calypso, reggae and steel pans (see resources page 82). Look out for steel pans performing at local schools or in your community.
* Explain that the steel pans are made from recycled oil drums. Help the children to 'find' items to recycle and turn in to musical instruments of their own. Use empty biscuit tins, baby milk tins and large coffee tins. Make beaters from wooden spoons. Prepare for a lot of noise!
* Add a selection of other instruments from the Caribbean (claves, bells, maracas, and guiro) to the metal drum band. Use your instruments to accompany Tropical Sunshine and In the Heat of the Caribbean Sun.

Taking it further

* Play with Boomwhackers (see resources page 83), pitched plastic pipes that make different notes when you tap them on the floor or each other.
* Collect together lots of empty crisp tubes with metal bases. Put a small bouncy rubber ball inside each and secure the lid with sticky tape. Shake them up and down and listen to the authentic steel pan sound that results.

With older children...

* Another musical sound of the Caribbean is the Tamboo Bamboo Band using hollow bamboo tubes hit or stamped on the ground. Use long cardboard or plastic tubes to tap on the ground in time to the beat as you sing some traditional songs such as

Songs and Games

Tropical Sunshine

Chant as a call and response song

Tropical sunshine (echo),
Tropical fruit (echo),
Tropical sounds (echo),
And the trumpets toot (echo).
Tropical islands (echo),
Tropical drums (echo),
Tropical dancing (echo),
And the rumba hums (echo).

In the Heat of the Caribbean Sun

Sing to the tune of *Brown Girl in the Ring*

Steel drums rumbling,
La la la la la.
Steel drums rumbling,

La la la la la la.
Steel drums rumbling,
La la la la la.
In the heat of the Caribbean sun.

Dancers tumbling,
La la la la la.
Dancers tumbling,
La la la la la la.
Dancers tumbling,
La la la la la.
In the heat of the Caribbean sun.

(Invite the children to add more verses to this song.)

Chinese Sound

Focus: experiment with the sounds of traditional Chinese music
and celebrate the new year!

Around
the World

What you need

* metal utensils, string, scissors, old metal musical instruments, metal beaters
* trolley. clothes stand or washing line
* pitched instruments, chime bars, metallophones, glockenspiels
* biscuit tin lids, wooden spoons, large plastic cylinders, leather or rubber for drum skins

Early Learning Goals

PSED: work as part of a group, taking turns and sharing fairly
CLL: extend their vocabulary, exploring the meaning and sounds of new words
KUW: begin to know their own cultures and beliefs and those of other people
PD: move with confidence, imagination and in safety

The Little Book of Sound Ideas

Activities

* Collect together lots of kitchen utensils such as metal saucepan lids, pots, spoons, whisks, sieves, chains. Add old triangles, cymbals or bells and suspend them on a trolley, clothes stand or washing line. Invite the children to tap them with a metal beater and create Chinese sounds.

* A lot of Chinese music uses the pentatonic or five note scale. Set up five chime bars or a metallophone using the notes C, D, E, G, A. Label them with their note. Let the children experiment or improvise with these notes. It will immediately sound eastern to our ears. Can they make up songs using the scale?

* Learn how to say 'Happy New Year' in Cantonese - 'Gung Hey Fat Choi'. Sing Gung Hey Fat Choi (see below).

* Make a Chinese Dragon Drum. Cover a large plastic or paper cylinder with red paper or paint. Make a skin for the drum using fabric, leather or a rubber inner tube. Use old biscuit tin lids hit with wooden spoons as gongs. Use these instruments to keep the beat as you walk slowly and solemnly around the room.

Taking it further

* Sing **Sound the Gong.** Encourage the children to take turns playing along with the gong.
* practice lining up a group of three or four children, each holding the shoulders of the child in front and going up and down as they bend their knees. Ask them to try moving under the material of the dragons tail. Invite some children to play the Chinese music using the metal sounds or gongs and drums.

With older children...

* Create a Chinese dragon dance. Construct a dragon head from a painted cardboard box and attach a very long piece of fabric for the tail. Listen to *Dragon Dance* (track 7 on *Music from The Little Book of Dance*).
* Play Catch the Tail. Ask the child at the head of the dragon to try and catch the child at the tail end without breaking the line!

Songs and Games

Gung Hey Fat Choi
Sing to the tune of *Seesaw Margery Daw*

Gung hey fat choi,
Happy new year to all of you.
Gung hey fat choi,
Happy new year to all of you.

Sound the Gong
Sing this song to the tune of *Frere Jacques*

Sound the gong,	X2
Hear it ring,	X2
Loud and strong,	X2
As you sing.	X2

Sound Symbols

Focus: finding out how to use simple notation of sounds

Storing Sounds

What you need

* selection of instruments and sound makers
* card, paper, whiteboards
* pens, crayons or paints

Early Learning Goals

PSED: maintain attention, concentrate and sit quietly when appropriate

CLL: know that print carries meaning

PSRN: talk about, recognise & recreate simple patterns

CD: express and communicate their ideas, thoughts and feelings by using widening range of materials and a variety of songs and musical instruments

Activities

This activity is better suited to older or more experienced children.

* Sit in a circle and give each child some paper or a small whiteboard and pens or crayons.
* Put a collection of instruments and sound makers in the centre of the circle. Make a sound and then invite the children to try to draw it. Encourage them to draw the sound rather than the instrument, for instance shaking a tambourine could just be wwwwww and tapping the claves could be x x x x .
* Now try it in reverse, draw some patterns and see if the children can interpret them using the instruments. Remember there is no right or wrong!
* Cut out cards and draw some of the symbols onto them. Allow children free play to use these cards and interpret the sounds. Can they play their piece to the group?
* Sort the instruments into groups according to materials such as: <u>skin</u> - drum, tambour, tambourine; <u>metal</u> - triangle, bells; <u>wood</u> - claves, woodblocks, some maracas, guiros; <u>plastic</u> - castanets, shakers. Make picture and word cards to label the groups.
* Give out the instruments around the circle in groups. Place the cards in front of each group. Invite a child to conduct (see Sound Makers on page 13) by standing by the card of the group they want to hear first and starting and stopping the sound.

Taking it further

* Sing A Wiggle Still Means 'sssssh'! using the children's drawings of different sounds. Ask each child in turn to choose a sound drawing for the next verse. Use instruments to make the sounds.
* Show them some actual rhythm notation. You could introduce a one beat note using a simple I or [♩] using a hand puppet. For example: Bill is a grumpy pirate who only cheers up when the children say and clap his name. Every time they see his note they have to say 'Bill' so ♩♩♩♩ will be 'Bill Bill Bill Bill'.
* Later you can introduce his parrot Lucy whose name is written like this [♫]. Before you know it you can be reading rhythms using the puppets' names [♩♫♩♫] = 'Bill Lucy Bill Lucy', etc.

Songs and Games

A Wiggle Still Means 'sssssh'!
If you see a star, [*]
It must be a crash.
But a wiggle still means 'sssssh'!

If you see a dot,
It must be a tap.
But a wiggle still means 'sssssh'!

If you see a zigzag,
It must be a shake.
But a wiggle still means 'sssssh'!

Soundscapes

Focus: using a variety of sounds to create sound pictures or soundscapes

Storing
Sounds

What you need

* large pieces of paper, coloured pencils and felt pens, glue
* musical instruments and sound makers
* long strips of paper such as lining paper or wall paper

Early Learning Goals

PSED: maintain attention, concentrate and sit quietly when appropriate

CLLD: use talk to organise, sequence and clarify thinking, ideas, feelings and events

PSRN: use everyday words to describe position

CD: use their imagination in art and design, music, dance, imaginative and role play and stories

The Little Book of Sound Ideas

Activities

* Ask the children to sit very quietly in a circle and listen to the sounds around them. What can they hear inside and outside the room?
* Inside the room they may notice breathing, a clock ticking, fidgeting, and so on. Outside the room, people talking, children playing, cars, footsteps, wind blowing, aeroplane, lawn mowers, etc.
* Explain that you are going to create a soundscape of your setting (see Day and Night Sounds on page 39 or Summer Sounds on page 49). Draw pictures of the sounds inside and outside the room. Ask the children to help you reproduce the sounds when you point at them using voices, body percussion and instruments.
* Sing Paint Me a Picture.
* Think about the sounds you might hear in other places such as the park, the high street or market, the swimming pool, their bedroom. Work with the children to collect ideas of groups of sounds. They can then choose a sound each to draw and use their pictures to create soundscapes by sticking them on long pieces of paper.

Taking it further

* Use pictures from magazines, posters, large photographs or paintings as scores to inspire sounds. Try using prints of landscape paintings by famous artists such as Monet, Turner, Van Gogh, and Hokusai. Talk about background sounds and foreground sounds.
* Invite the children to paint on big pieces of paper as they listen to different moods of music. If the music is very loud what does the painting look like?
* Listen to *Pictures at an Exhibition* by Mussorgsky. These pieces were inspired by a series of paintings. Can the children imagine what the pictures were like?

With older children...

* Invite the children to use their drawings or pictures from magazines or junk mail as a score to conduct from. Help them to point at different parts of the picture and organise the sounds. Will all the sounds happen one by one or could they all happen at the same time?

Songs and Games

Paint Me a Picture
Sing to the tune of *Dance to Your Daddy*

Paint me a picture,   X3
Using lots of sounds.
Loud and quiet,
High and low,

Long and short,
Fast and slow.
Paint me a picture,   X3
Using lots of sounds.

Making Sound Boxes

Focus: use these sets of recycled junk materials as resources for small groups to create sounds

Storing Sounds

What you need

* large plastic stacking boxes, paper, tape or glue, pens
* junk! - see activities for suggestions

Ask children, parents, colleagues and other adults to help you collect a good range of junk items for your sound boxes. You could place a large collecting box near the entrance to your setting and ask adults to bring in useful items.

Early Learning Goals

PSED: continue to be interested, excited and motivated to learn;

CLLD: use talk to organise, sequence and clarify thinking, ideas, feelings and events; attempt writing for various purposes

PD: use a range of small and large equipment

CD: express and communicate their ideas, thoughts and feelings by using a widening range of materials and musical instruments

The Little Book of Sound Ideas

Activities

* Collect lots of junk materials for making music. Work together to sort them into groups. Examples of items and their suggested groups are listed below.
* Once the children have decided on the groups for sorting the junk into they can make labels for the boxes. Labels can be pictures, words, photographs or a combination of these.
* Here are some suggestions of sound box groups and the junk items that may be in each box for children to create their own instruments:

Drums - metal based tins with plastic lids such as cocoa, baby milk, gravy powder, crisp tubes, biscuit tins and lids; upturned plastic buckets (all sizes); water fountain bottles.

Beaters - sets of wooden, plastic or metal spoons, sticks, pencils, dowels.

Tappers - pairs of lids from fabric softener bottles or aerosols, empty yogurt pots or drinks bottles, film canisters.

Shakers - variety mini-cereal boxes, small drink bottles, washing up liquid or other small plastic bottles, salt shakers, sweet containers and film canisters; small pebbles, sand, dry rice or beans and coloured water for fillings, clear adhesive film or wrapping paper.

Jinglers - bells, shells, metal bottle tops, washers, string.

Scrapers - plastic soapboxes, squares of corrugated cardboard, ridged plastic boxes, polystyrene vegetable and fruit trays, large clear ridged squash bottles (can double up as shakers too), blocks to cover with sandpaper, loofahs.

Scrunchers - plastic biscuit and cake trays make a great scrunchy sound when squashed but don't last very long!

Blowers - small plastic bottles without lids to blow across.

* Sing What's In the Sound Box? and Use Them All to Make a Row.

Taking it further

* You can use all or some of these resources to create a junk orchestra with the children. Try recording some of the different sounds. Try lots of different combinations. Have fun!

With older children...

* Make labels for the boxes using your computer.

Songs and Games

What's In the Sound Box?

Sing to the tune of *My Old Man's a Dustman*

What's in the sound box?
What's in it today?
What's in the sound box?
What are we going to play?
There are tappers in the sound box,
In the box today.

Tappers in the sound box.
That's what we're going to play!

Use Them All to Make a Row!

Don't let those bottles go to waste.
Don't crush the empty tins.
Don't throw away those boxes.
Don't put them in the bins.
No way, no how!

Use them all to make a row!

Don't let those pots go to rot.
Don't squash those tubes flat.
Don't rip the cardboard up.
Don't do that!
No way, no how!
Use them all to make a row!

Sound Corner

Focus: this should be a permanent feature of your setting, where children can make and listen to music independently

Storing Sounds

What you need

* small easy chairs, big and small cushions, bean bags, throws
* a supply of varied tapes and CDs with a wide range of styles of music and stories
* a collection of musical instruments and sound makers

Early Learning Goals

PSED: form good relationships with adults & peers
CLLD: listen with enjoyment and respond to stories, songs and other music, rhymes and poems and make up their own stories, songs, rhymes and poems;
KUW: find out about and identify the uses of everyday technology and use information and communication technology
CD: respond in a variety of ways to what they see, hear, smell, touch and feel

The Little Book of Sound Ideas

Activities

* Work with the children to decide on the best place to have a permanent sound corner where they can listen to or make sounds.
* Offer comfortable chairs, cushions and bean bags so that children can make themselves cosy. Add a radio, tape recorder or CD player and headphones.
* Provide a varied selection of music: children's songs, classical music, world music, jazz, folk, etc. Invite the children to bring in favourite tapes or CDs of music or stories from home to share with the group. Change the music regularly.
* Add lots of story tapes and books for children who prefer to listen to a story.
* Don't forget to include recordings made by the children themselves.
* As a group, decide on the rules for the sound corner, for example, sound levels so that others are not disturbed.
* Promote listening as an enjoyable activity. Choose one tape to be Music or Story of the Week and encourage as many children as possible to listen to it. Talk about it at snack time.
* Provide the children with different instruments or sound makers to experiment with. Change the resources regularly so there is always a new sound to discover.

Taking it further

* Have an opening for your new sound corner. Send invitations, decorate the space, make snacks, cut the ribbon, sing Come in Here and other songs suggested by the children, have a party!
* Invite visitors to come and talk to the children about listening to music and share their top five songs. Invite the children to choose a piece of music to talk about to the group.
* Try inviting some musicians and create some live music in the sound corner!

With older children...

* Encourage the children to develop their sound corner by adding signs, suggesting organisation and keeping a record of their favourite music, songs and stories.

Songs and Games

Come in Here

Sing to the tune of *Michael Row the Boat Ashore*

Come in here and listen now,
Alleluia.

Come in here and listen now,
Alleluia.

Come in here and make some sounds,
Alleluia.

Come in here and make some sounds,
Alleluia.

The Little Book of Sound Ideas

Recording Studio

Focus: use simple equipment to allow children to experiment with recording sounds

Storing Sounds

What you need

* portable or home-made screen, tape recorder, microphones, stands, musical instruments and sound makers, blank tapes, chairs and cushions
* table or desk, chair, computer (optional), telephone, paper, diary, pens, etc

Early Learning Goals

PSED: select and use activities and resources independently

CLLD: use language to imagine and recreate roles and experiences; attempt writing for different purposes, using features of different forms such as lists, stories and instructions

KUW: find out about and identify the uses of everyday technology and use information and communication technology

The Little Book of Sound Ideas

Activities

* Set up a role play area as a recording studio. Use screens to create the effect of soundproofing. Put out easy to operate tape recorders with built-in microphones, pretend microphones, musical instruments, blank tapes, sheet music, comfortable chairs, and cushions.
* Add a front office with a desk, diary and telephone to make bookings.
* Show the children how to operate the recording equipment.
* Show them how to record their voices, talking or singing. Listen back. Can they identify themselves or their friends?
* Encourage them to make up their own songs and sounds to record.
* Make signs for the studio such as 'Recording', 'Please be quiet', 'Come back later'.
* Make a listening quiz - by recording sounds of familiar instruments for others to recognise.
* Record the children singing Make the Song Your Own.

Taking it further

* Use a video recorder to film the children playing in the recording studio.
* Use junk materials to make pretend microphones with cardboard tubes, sponge balls, glue, black and silver paint, etc.
* Put a tape or CD player outside. Provide music and microphones for outdoor karaoke.

With older children...

* Invite a musician to visit and talk about their experiences in the studio.
* Ask children to work in pairs and choose two different sounds. Try playing them one after the other and then both at the same time. Record the sounds together. Can the group identify both the sounds? What happens when you play or record more than two instruments at a time?
* Use the Recording Studio as a radio station, where children can record themselves introduce songs or interview each other and you!

Songs and Games

Make the Song Your Own
Sing this song to the tune of *Oh My Darling*

Make a sound,
Make it now,
Sing into the microphone.
Press the buttons,
Watch it whirring,
And make the song your own.

Make a new sound,
Change the words,
Sing into the microphone.
Press the buttons,
Watch it whirring,
And make the song your own.

Tap a rhythm,
Shake a pattern,
Sing into the microphone....

Sounds and Words

More with Sounds

What you need

* pieces of card cut in the shape of speech bubbles
* paper, magazines, pens, crayons, paints, glue

Early Learning Goals

CLLD: explore and experiment with sounds, words and texts; respond to rhymes and poems and make up their own rhymes and poems; extend their vocabulary, exploring the meaning and sounds of new words

CD: express and communicate their ideas, thoughts and feelings by using a widening range of materials

Activities

This activity is better suited to older or more experienced children.

* Talk about sound words. Make a list of words that describe sounds such as rattle, ring, bang, ding, hiss, boom, ching, etc. Write them on pieces of card, or stick on letters cut from magazines. Hang them around the room. Encourage children to use them in their play.
* Sing Can You Sing my Song? and Singing Sounds.
* Make up sound poems with the children. Help them to think of rhyming strings such as 'ring ding ching', 'boom doom zoom' and 'tap clap zap'. Don't worry if they make up 'new' words, just let the children explore the sounds of the rhyming words.
* Play with alliterations and create descriptive phrases. Can the children make a 'hurried hiss', 'short shake', 'dull ding', 'big bang' or a 'cheerful ching'?
* Make rhyming lines by collecting together as many rhymes as possible in one sentence, for instance - 'the fat cat sat on the mat in a hat, fancy that' or 'the dog went for a jog in the fog and met a hog by a log'.

Taking it further

* Collect together phrases and sayings about sound and talk about them to the children, eg 'as quiet as mice', 'as clear as a bell' and 'for crying out loud'.
* Make sound word calligrams (a word written to look like its meaning). Choose a word that describes a sound and print or write it out in different ways. Invite the children to decorate the words with drawings and cuttings of pictures that relate to the word, so 'loud' could be in very big letters, with spiky zigzags all around, and pictures of drums, guitars, people shouting, machines, etc. 'Ding' could be in wobbly letters, with bells, triangles, telephones, etc.

Songs and Games

Can You Sing my Song?
Sing to the tune of *My Old Man's a Dustman*

Rattle, rattle, prattle,
Ring ding, dang ding, dong,
Click clack crunch,
Clang clap munch,
Can you sing my song?

Can you add more sound words
As you sing along?
Bing bang boom,
Zing zong zoom,
Can you sing my song?

Singing Sounds
Sing to the tune of
Skip to my Lou

Ringing bells, ding, ding, ding,   X3
Sing the sounds together.

Rattling bones, rattle, rattle, rattle,   X3
Sing the sounds together.

Flapping fish, flap, flap, flap, etc.
Popping corn, pop, pop, pop, etc.
Banging door, bang, bang, bang, etc.

Sounds and Numbers

Focus: using number skills to explore and have fun with sounds

More with Sounds

What you need

* large dice or cube boxes (such as tissue boxes)
* selection of instruments and sound makers
* pieces of card, pens, scissors

Early Learning Goals

PSED: work as part of a group or class, taking turns and sharing fairly

CLLD: make up their own songs, rhymes & poems

PSRN: count reliably up to ten everyday objects; recognise numerals 1-9

KUW: find out about and identify the uses of everyday technology

CD: recognise repeated sounds

The Little Book of Sound Ideas

Activities

* Choose an instrument each and sit in a circle to play these dice games.
* Let the dice decide how many times you play each instrument or make a sound. Sing Roll the Dice.
* Choose six different instruments or sounds and label them with the numbers one - six. Take turns to roll the dice to see which sound to play. Roll again to see how many times to make the sound.
* Make some number cards using the numbers one to six. Ask a child to pick two or three cards and play the instruments that are labelled with those numbers.
* Play Sound Bingo. Make cards showing four or more sound sources, instruments, animals, machines, or sound words. Use recorded or live sounds and ask the children to listen carefully and put a counter over the sound when they have heard it.
* Sing and play instruments for the number songs Play Two Sounds and I'm Gonna Play.

Taking it further

* Sing lots of well-known action number rhymes such as *Five Fat Sausages*, *Five Brown Buns*, *Five Fat Peas* and *Five Little Ducks*. Make up some new rhymes using these as models. Try *Five Fast Motor Cars* or *Five Yellow Bananas*. Encourage the children to come up with ideas for words and actions.

With older children...

* Put out three hoops and sort the instruments into sets. Put all the instruments that you tap in one circle, all the instruments you scrape into another, and all the ones you shake into a third. Position the rings so that those instruments that you can tap and shake eg the tambourine, can go in the overlap. Number each section. Throw the dice and play an instrument from that section.

Songs and Games

Roll the Dice

Sing to the tune of *Deck the Halls*

Roll the dice and count the dots,
How many sounds shall I make?
Roll the dice and count the spots,
It's your turn to give them a shake.

Play Two Sounds

Sing to the tune of *Hot Cross Buns*

Play two sounds,   X2
Play two sounds together.
Play two sounds.

Play three sounds,   X2
One after the other.
Play three sounds.

(Try with different numbers of sounds)

I'm Gonna Play

Sing to the tune of *Dem Bones*

I'm gonna play just - one sound,   x3
Can you hear my sound?

I'm gonna play just - two sounds,   X3
Can you hear my sounds?

Sounds in a Book

Focus: looking at books of sounds and making their own lift the flap book

More with Sounds

What you need

* a selection of story or lift-the-flap books about sounds (see activities on opposite page for suggestions)
* sugar paper, paints, felt pens, glue
* lots of different types of paper

Early Learning Goals

PSED: work as part of a group or class, taking turns and sharing fairly

CLLD: listen with enjoyment and respond to stories, and make up their own stories; show an understanding of the elements of stories

KUW: select the tools and techniques they need to shape, assemble and join materials they are using

The Little Book of Sound Ideas

Activities

* Share books about sounds such as *Hattie's House* by Mandy and Ness (Little Hippo), *Who's Making That Noise?* by Stephen Cartwright (Usborne) and *Spot's Noisy Walk* by Eric Hill (Frederick Warne). Enjoy lifting the flaps and guessing who is making the sounds.

* Talk to the children about making your own book of sounds. Choose a character to hear the sounds. It could be a child, an animal or a favourite toy. Decide who or what is really making the sounds, this character or item should go under the flaps. Ask children to draw or paint pictures for the book. Put the book in the book or sound corner (see page 69) so that children can enjoy looking through it and making the sounds.

* Sing Sound File Chant. Act out some of the lines from the poem. Can the children think of some more? Work together to invent a new sound file about your setting.

Taking it further

* Play Hello Goodbye. Ask for a volunteer to stand on their own with their eyes covered and listen as another child from the group greets them. Can they identify the speaker? What happens if the voice is disguised?

With older children...

* How many different sounds can the children make using paper? Provide them with a selection of paper: newspaper, aluminium foil, tissue paper, card, paper bags, cardboard tubes and boxes, egg cartons, etc. Ask them to experiment by tapping, tearing, scrunching, blowing and shaking. Sing Paper Music.

* Read a story that the children know well. Choose a voice, body or instrument sound for each of the main characters. Read the story again and make each character's noise each time you read out his or her name.

Songs and Games

Sound File Chant

Baby crying.
Mum sighing.
Sister laughing.
Brother talking.
TV blaring.
Dad snoring.
Cat washing.
Dog eating.
Clock ticking.
Phone ringing.
You speaking.
Me singing.

Paper Music

Sing to the tune of *Mix the Pancake*

Tear the paper,
Crunch the paper,
Fold it in a crease.
Blow the paper,
Scrape the paper.
Please leave me a piece?

Sound with Moves

Focus: try out these musical movement games using live and recorded sounds

Sounds etc...

What you need

* a large space
* hoops, lengths of ribbon, tinsel, net, chiffon, sticks, curtain rings, hair bobbles (wear around wrists), etc
* a variety of recorded dance music
* a selection of musical instruments

Early Learning Goals

PSED: have a developing respect for their own cultures and beliefs and those of other people

PD: move with control and coordination; show awareness of space, of themselves and of others; recognise the changes that happen to their bodies when they are active

CD: use their imagination in dance

The Little Book of Sound Ideas

Activities

* Try an aerobics session. Choose some recorded dance music with a strong beat. Ask the children to spread out and stand well-spaced out in the space. Warm up by circling the shoulders and marching on the spot. Then try stepping forwards and backwards in time to the beat. Bend from side to side, take four steps left and then to the right. Keep it simple.
* Add equipment such as hoops, ribbons, tinsel etc. to the aerobics session.
* Stand in a circle and play Traffic Lights. Choose three different sounds to represent the three lights, for instance shaken castanet = stop (stand still), maracas = get ready (walk up and down on the spot), claves = move (walk or trot).
* Sing and dance to Dance Dance and Dance Around the Room.

Taking it further

* Play some well-known musical party games such as Musical Statues and Musical Bumps. Add variety by asking the children to stand very tall, or balance on one leg or make a spiky statue, or to bump onto their bottom, knees, back or tummy, or find a friend to hug, when the music stops.
* Play Simon's Sound. You could also try movement songs and games such as *The Bear Went Over the Mountain, We All Clap Hands Together, The Okey-Cokey* and *Here we go Looby Lou.*

With older children...

* Watch some video of different styles of dancing from around the world.
* Make a collection of recorded dance music to listen and move to. Choose lots of different styles to suit a variety of moods (see Resources on page 81). Allow the children some time to freely interpret the music. Teach them a few simple steps. Try tap dancing - toe, toe, heel heel, toe - or a simple waltz - step with the left, step with the right, feet together.
* Make ribbons or streamers by attaching ribbon to short pieces of doweling, curtain rings or hair bobbles. Alternatively, use tinsel to sparkle like fireworks, rain or for Christmas celebrations.
* Use different coloured chiffon scarves and dance to *Colours of the Wind* from Pocahontas.

Songs and Games

Simon's Sound

- *Simon Says* using sounds.

Explain that the children should try to copy your actions but only if the action is preceded by an agreed sound signal. Shake a tambourine before each movement you want them to copy. Try and catch them out by leaving out the sound signal or playing the wrong sound!

Dance to Your Daddy (traditional)

Dance Dance

Sing to the tune of *Lord of the Dance*

Dance, dance wherever you may be.
Dancing is fun as you soon will see.
Take my hand and dance with me.
Dancing is fun as you soon will see.

Dance Around the Room

Sing to the tune of *Polly Put the Kettle on*

Dance around the room with me,   X3
Let's all dance.

Resources

Songs and rhymes to support the activities in this book

Away in a Manger
Brown Girl in the Ring
Dance to Your Daddy
Deck the Halls
Diddle Diddle Dumpling
Dingle-Dangle Scarecrow
Five Brown Buns
Five Fat Peas
Five Fat Sausages
Five Little Ducks
Five Little Speckled Frogs
Heads, Shoulders, Knees and Toes
Here We Go Looby Lou
Here We Go Round the
Mulberry Bush
Hush Little Baby
I Can Sing a Rainbow

If You're Happy and You Know it
In a Dark, Dark Wood
I See the Moon
I Went to School One Morning
I Went to the Garden and Dug
Up the Ground
I Went to Visit a Farm One Day
Jingle Bells
Old MacDonald Had a Farm
Peter Hammers with One
Hammer
Raindrops Keep Falling on My
Head
Rock a Bye Baby
Row, Row Row Your Boat
Rudolph, the Red Nosed
Reindeer

Skip to My Lou
Star Light, Star Bright
Start Your Day
The Animal Fair
The Bear Went Over the Mountain
The Big Ship Sails on the Alley
Alley O
The Farmer's in His Den
The Grand Old Duke of York
The Okey-Cokey
Tinga Layo
Twinkle, Twinkle Little Star
Two Little Dicky-Birds
We All Clap Hands Together
Yellow Bird

The words for many of these songs and rhymes are available in the following books and website:

Songs for the Early Years	Jean Evans (Compiler)	Kevin Mayhew	1844171809
The Little Book of Nursery Rhymes	Sally Featherstone (Compiler)	Featherstone Education	1904187536
Merrily to Bethlehem: 44 Christmas Songs and Carols for Children,	David Gadsby and Ivor Golby (Editors)	A&C Black	0713667516
Nursery Rhyme Songbook	Caroline Hooper (Compiler)	Usborne Songbooks	0746017030
Brown Girl in the Ring: An Anthology of Song Games from the Eastern Caribbean,	Alan Lomax et al (Compilers)	Pantheon Books	0679404538
This Little Puffin	Elizabeth Matterson (Compiler)	Puffin Books	
Movement Plus Rhymes, Songs and Singing Games	Phyllis S. Weikart	High/Scope Press	1573790664

www.flyingpigs.org.uk/songs - this site is packed with campfire songs. Be aware that even the youngest Beaver Scouts are 6 and so many of the songs may be too difficult, but if you are looking for the lyrics to a specific song then Dave and Pam Eason's A-Z listings make it easy to find. Also includes some interesting craft activities.

More sources of songs, rhymes and music games suitable for children in the Foundation Stage

Okki-Tokki-Unga: Action Songs for Children	Beatrice Harrop (Editor)	A & C Black	0713640782
Bobby Shaftoe Clap Your Hands: Musical Fun with New Songs from Old	Sue Nicholls	A & C Black	0713635568
Seasons: Songs for 4-7 Year Olds	Ana Sanderson	A & C Black	0713648015
Hey Diddle Diddle and other nursery rhymes		Ladybird Books	1844223167
Humpty Dumpty and other nursery rhymes		Ladybird Books	0721420184
Incy Wincy Spider and other nursery rhymes		Ladybird Books	1844223159

Music to support the activities in this book

Sandpaper Ballet	Leroy Anderson (The Best of)	Universal
Lullaby	Johannes Brahms	Eclipse
Pictures at an Exhibition	Modest Mussorgsky	Naxos
Carnival of the Animals	Camille Saint-Saens	Arion records
The Nutcracker Suite	Pyotr Tchaikovsky (narrated by Prunella Scales)	Naxos
Four Seasons	Antonio Vivaldi	Naxos
Singing in the Rain	Various	Platinum records

Colours of the Wind from Pocahontas, Under the Sea from The Little Mermaid and Little April Showers from Bambi are all available on:

Ultimate Disney	Various Artists	Wsm

More music suitable for children in the Foundation Stage

Carousel	Linda Caroe	Carousel*
Small Voices, Big Noises	Martin Harwood and Quentin Rawlings	Featherstone Education
Music for the Little Book of Dance	Brian Madigan	Featherstone Education
Children's Favourite Songs	Various Artists	Walt Disney
No Music for the Early Years? No Problem?		Kevin Mayhew*

* Available from Featherstone Education.

Natural Sounds

A wide range of Audio CDs focusing on natural sounds are available from music labels such as Oreade Music (Sounds of the Earth series), Laserlight (Echos of Nature series) Reflection and Delta. Sounds include the sea, the rainforest, thunderstorms, birds, dolphins and frog chorus.

World Sounds

www.roughguides.co.uk/music - Series includes African and Latin music for children, Australian Aboriginal music; music from India, Ireland, and china; calypso, reggae and jazz.

Some sound books to start your collection

Who's Making that Noise?	Stephen Cartwright	Usborne	0746008503
The Singing Sack: 28 Song-stories from Around the World	Helen East	A & C Black	0713658053
Sing Me a Story!: Song and Dance Stories from the Caribbean	Grace Hallworth	Frances Lincoln	071121851X
Spot's Noisy Walk	Eric Hill	Fredrick Warne	0785326812
Hatties' House	Mandy and Ness	Little Hippo	1840591536
Newton	Rory Tyger	Little Tiger Press	1854307215
Snappy Sounds - Farm: Noisy Pop-up Fun		Templar	1840113804

Musical resources

ASCO
19 Lockwood Way, Leeds. LS11 5TH
0113 270 7070 www.ascoeducational.co.uk
Range includes percussion packs, colourful animal themed instruments and traditional looking instruments from around the world.

Eduzone
29 Friern Barnet Road, London. N11 1NE
08456 445 556 www.eduzone.co.uk
Boomwhackers, ocean drums and wrist and ankle bells feature among their wide range of musical instruments.

Spacekraft
Titus House, 29 Saltaire Road, Shipley, West Yorkshire. BD18 3HH
01274 581007 www.spacekraft.co.uk
drums, wooden percussion, shakers, guiros, rain sticks and kazoos.

WESCO
Burnham Way, Queens Bridge Road, Nottingham. NG2 1NB
0115 986 2126 sales@wesco.co.uk
wide range of musical instruments including rainsticks, kokirikos and musical dominoes as well as the more traditional.

These suppliers also offer solutions to comfortable seating for your sound corner.

2to5.com
PO Box 821, Peterborough, Cambridgeshire. PE1 9AF
01733 808 003 www.2to5.com
RSPB Audubon Birds - visually recognisable soft toy birds that make the same sound as real birds.

Lycra Squares for dance, waterproofs and whiteboards are all available from Featherstone Education
01858 881212 www.feathestone.uk.com

Sketches for Summer Sounds (page 50)

Use these sketches to illustrate the movement and shapes of the play equipment that the children may have seen at the local park or playground during the Summer Sounds activity on page 50. Encourage the children to make the same patterns with their voices: up the steps and swoop down the slide; slide the voice gently up and down on the swing; very high and very low to create the seesaw; round and round on the roundabout.

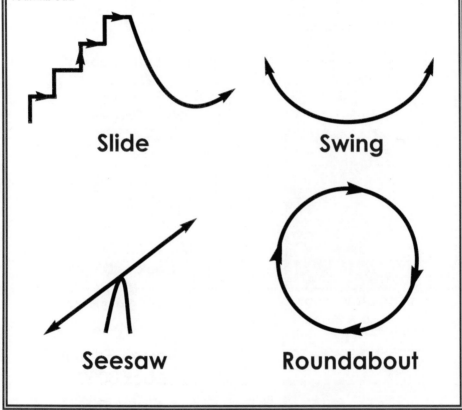

Slide

Swing

Seesaw

Roundabout

If you have found this book useful you might also like ...

The Little Book of Music
LB16
ISBN 1-904187-54-4

The Little Book of Dance
LB33
ISBN 1-904187-74-9

The Little Book of Junk Music
LB26
ISBN 1-904187-87-0

Music for The Little Book of Dance (CD)
ISBN 1-904187-17-X

All available from

Featherstone Education
PO Box 6350
Lutterworth
LE17 6ZA
T:0185 888 1212
F:0185 888 1360

on our web site

www.featherstone.uk.com

and from selected book suppliers

Small Voices, Big Noises (CD)
ISBN 1-904187-56-0